"Where atheists see only aimless natural processes many religious thinkers find detailed design. Drawing upon his years of careful analyses, Haught challenges both of these groups to look deeper, to see neither a purposeless universe nor carefully controlled craftwork by an intervening God, to recognize instead a cosmic drama. The story of the universe continues to unfold, the plotlines are often blurred, and the outcome remains a puzzle. As Teilhard already saw, nonetheless, the sequence of cosmic, biological, and human social evolution suggests a goal-oriented direction, emerging from a source deeper than an intervening Designer, a source continuously calling the universe forward. Haught provides a clear and provocative theological vision adequate to the grandeur of the universe science describes."
> —Michael H. Barnes, Professor, Religious Studies, President
> of the College Theology Society 2008–2010, University of Dayton

"Haught, a scientifically well-informed theologian and a leader in the emerging field of evolutionary theology, deflates the simplistic theology of materialists with a lucid account of where God fits in the drama of evolution. Science and theology are not competitors or alternatives, but complementary ways of knowing complementary things about reality. Built around the idea of layered explanation, this book will be a boon to everyone who struggles to make sense of how God might act in the world."
> —Daryl P. Domning, Professor of Anatomy, Howard University,
> and Research Associate, Department of Paleobiology, National Museum
> of Natural History, Smithsonian Institution, Washington, DC

"In contemporary debates on the theory of evolution, the process of natural selection has been often opposed to divine creativity. Professor John Haught in his search for the deep meaning of evolutionary mechanisms overcomes this facile opposition and develops a fascinating explanatory proposal in which both the laws of nature and the creating God play important roles in the process of evolutionary growth. Haught in a masterful way presents his vision of evolution in which scientific examination of evolutionary processes discloses divinity hidden in the evolving nature. This is a very important book that eliminates the tension between the natural and the religious dimension of events. Consequently—*extra naturam nulla salus*—there is no salvation outside of the created world. An evolutionary descendant of an amoeba has been endowed not only with an extraordinary gift of reflection, but also with a possibility to participate in God's life."
> —Archbishop Józef Życiński, Professor of Philosophy,
> University of Lublin, Poland; author of *God and Evolution*

Making Sense of Evolution

Making Sense of Evolution

Darwin, God,
and the Drama of Life

JOHN F. HAUGHT

WESTMINSTER
JOHN KNOX PRESS
LOUISVILLE · KENTUCKY

First edition
Published by Westminster John Knox Press
Louisville, KY

11 12 13 14 15 16 17 18 19—10 9 8 7 6 5 4 3

Except as otherwise indicated, Scripture quotations are from the New Revised Standard Version of the Bible, and are copyright © 1989 by the Division of Christian Education of the National Council of the Churches of Christ in the U.S.A., and are used by permission.

Scripture quotations marked NASB are taken from the *New American Standard Bible,* © 1960, 1962, 1963, 1968, 1971, 1972, 1973, 1975, 1977 by The Lockman Foundation. Used by permission.

Scripture quotations marked NIV are from *The Holy Bible, New International Version.* Copyright © 1973, 1978, 1984 International Bible Society. Used by permission of Zondervan Bible Publishers.

Book design by Sharon Adams
Cover design by designpointinc.com
Cover illustration: istockphoto.com

Library of Congress Cataloging-in-Publication Data

Haught, John F.
  Making sense of evolution : Darwin, God, and the drama of life / John F. Haught.
    p. cm.
  Includes index.
  ISBN 978-0-664-23285-6 (alk. paper)
  1. Evolution—Religious aspects—Christianity.   I. Title.
  BT712.H383 2010
  231.7'652—dc22

                                                    2009033748

To my sons
Paul and Martin

Contents

Acknowledgments

I wish to thank Westminster John Knox Press for the opportunity to introduce and develop my theological reflections on the endlessly fascinating and increasingly important topic of evolution. I am especially grateful to Executive Editor Donald McKim for his kind encouragement throughout 2009, the year during which I composed the following meditations on the story of life, and the period that marked the 200th anniversary of Charles Darwin's birthday. Thanks also to Daniel Braden for his many helpful editorial suggestions. I am also indebted to my paleontologist friend Daryl Domning for reading the manuscript and offering helpful suggestions. Most of all, thanks to my wife Evelyn for her constant encouragement.

I am dedicating this book to my sons Paul and Martin for the depth and dramatic beauty they have added to their parents' lives.

Introduction

> *No other modern work has done so much to change man's concept of himself and the universe in which he lives.*
> —George Gaylord Simpson, referring to Charles Darwin's
> On the Origin of Species[1]

*E*volution makes very good sense scientifically, but does it make sense theologically? This book is an invitation to Charles Darwin and his disciples to join in a conversation with contemporary Christian theology on the question of what evolution means for our understanding of God and what we take to be God's creation.

Darwin would surely be shocked to learn that, two hundred years after his birth, he is being asked to participate in such an exchange. Possibly you're surprised as well. Wasn't Darwin the archenemy of theology? Didn't his strange new ideas wipe from the natural record everything previous generations of Christians had taken to be evidence of an almighty, beneficent creator? Why place Darwin in the company of theologians? Or, as many of his friends might ask, why have him engage in dialogue with such a disreputable lot? In any case, isn't Darwin a threat not only to creationists and proponents of intelligent design (ID) but also to anyone who believes in a personal, creative, wise, providential, redemptive God?

As we begin a response to these questions, it is important to remind ourselves that Darwin was never an atheist. He eventually settled into a rather reluctant agnosticism some years after his famous sea voyage (1831–36), but he never formally renounced belief in a creator. At times he spoke of God in order to account for the existence of the inviolable laws of nature. True, Darwin's God remains remote from our everyday life and is uninvolved in the details of natural and human history, but Darwin never railed against Christianity in the feverish manner of the recent "new atheism" of Christopher

Hitchens or Richard Dawkins. Although he rejected some important Christian teachings, he devised no project to undermine the faith of his fellow humans. Indeed, he had the deepest sympathy and respect for acquaintances who found consolation in their creeds, not least his devout wife, Emma. It is not unlikely that he too longed for the comfort of faith even as it drifted irreversibly away from him.

Darwin eventually arrived at a point in his religious odyssey where, if he entertained the idea of God at all, it was an idea that provided little comfort. His lukewarm "deism," his belief in a dispassionate first cause of the cosmos, is not enough to justify the invitation I am extending to him here. In fact, his explicit theological understanding is extremely lean, preoccupied as it is with the narrow idea of God as an intelligent designer. Given his religiously watery concept of God, one that he shared with countless other educated skeptics of his day, it is not hard to understand why he moved away from Christianity as he understood it.

So why should Christian theologians warmly embrace him as a conversation partner today? Partly because his scientific writings, as we shall see, never worked themselves completely free of Darwin's own theological preoccupations. But mostly because of the enormous implications that his science of "evolution" has for Christian teachings, especially the doctrines of creation, providence, and redemption. During all the Christian centuries, it is doubtful that any set of ideas has challenged theology or provoked believers in a more disquieting manner than those of Darwin. Hence, theologians today would do well to keep him involved in any serious interpretations of their fundamental beliefs. It may turn out that his presence among theologians will challenge—and sharpen—their reflections more dramatically even than Copernicus and Galileo had done earlier.

For a moment, just ponder Darwin's claim that all life on earth has descended from a single common ancestor that lived ages ago, an idea not original with him but one that is fundamental to his science. What does his idea of common ancestry mean for our understanding of life, of who we are, and of what our relationship with the rest of nature should be? Or consider Darwin's idea of "natural selection," the impersonal winnowing mechanism responsible for the emergence of new species over an unimaginably immense span of time. If all the diverse species arose gradually by way of a blind natural process, in what sense can God still be called the author of life, if at all? And if our own species is a product of natural selection, can Christian theologians still responsibly pass on the news that we are created in the "image" and "likeness" of God (Gen. 1:26)? Since human beings apparently evolved as one species among others, what does this imply for our ideas about the soul, original sin, and salvation? And what does "Christ" mean if Jesus also is a product of evolution?

Darwin dropped a religiously explosive bomb into the Victorian culture of his contemporaries, and Christians ever since—including some, though certainly not all, theologians—have been scrambling either to defuse it or toss it out of harm's way. Meanwhile, scientific skeptics claim that the device has already gone off, shattering for good the hollow babbling of religions and making the world finally safe for atheism.

Darwin's "dangerous idea," we shall see, is much less lethal than all that, but there can be no doubt that it is theologically consequential. If the atheist philosopher Daniel Dennett is right, Darwin's theory of evolution is like a "universal acid."[2] It dissolves everything people have thought to be solid, including ethics, religion, and intelligence, explaining them as mere adaptations serving the interest of "selfish genes." If that were the case, it would also subvert any claims made by Dennett's own mind, exposing that organ also as a mere adaptation, and hence not worth taking seriously by lovers of truth. But even so, evolution is an interruption that theology has to face with more candor than in the past. Darwin's revolution is a cold bath that should shock theologians into an exceptional state of alertness, bracing them for a whole new religious adventure.

So Darwin deserves an invitation to any serious theological conversation, today more than ever. I realize that wary readers will immediately protest that Darwin's "evolutionary theory" has yet to be proved, it is "merely" a theory, sufficient evidence for it is lacking, and nobody has ever "seen" life evolving. Opponents of Darwin will claim that the fossil record is incomplete, radiometric dating is flawed, the origin of every new species is a miraculous event, natural selection is a tautology, accidents are not real. Some will plea that, even today, theology is wasting its time taking seriously the wild ideas of a misguided nineteenth-century naturalist from Downe, England.

Along with evolutionary biologists and science educators, I confess to a certain impatience with such groundless objections to Darwin's carefully constructed theory. I am even tempted here to quote an old Jesuit who, when asked about the evidence for evolution, replied in frustration, "The very fact that monkeys have hands is enough to give us paws." But since I am not a Jesuit, I shall refrain from dragging the reader down into such depths this early in our inquiry.

Anyway, dismissing evolution offhand after two centuries of reliable research by sciences ranging from geology to genetics smacks of ignorance and arrogance unbecoming to people of faith. I am not a scientist, but I am fully aware that knowledgeable people now almost universally accept Darwin's version of evolution as updated by the discovery of the units of heredity known as genes. Like all scientific ideas, the theory is open to improvement or even falsification if the evidence leads in that direction, but so far it has withstood every test. Only rarely will you find a maverick scientist here and there who rejects it; the great majority of educated people in the world today accept evolution, even if they are not always happy about it. Many, if not most, Christian theologians likewise assent to the theory. The same is true of high ecclesiastics. In 1996 Pope John Paul II, for example, observed that the evidence for evolution is strong, and many other religious leaders concur.

Nevertheless, a century and a half after *The Origin of Species* first appeared, I doubt that a completely candid conversation between Christian theologians and Darwin has yet to occur. Such an undertaking may take several more generations of continuing dialogue. The most I can do in the following pages is to provide a sketch of how a substantive discussion between Darwin and Christian theology might begin. My project is a quite limited one. I cannot say how Muslims, Jews, Hindus, and Buddhists will deal with Darwin, although perhaps even they may take a little bit from the reflections that follow. My own focus, however, will be on the conversation of Darwin with Christian theology.

Darwin was not always at ease conversing with theologians, but I shall take advantage of the fact that in his own lifetime he was already involved in serious theological discussion with some of his friends and correspondents, uncomfortable though he often was with such exchanges. Even if his own contributions to these conversations were increasingly those of a skeptic, he could not deny that his work had dramatic theological implications, including the possibility that traditional theology would be rendered obsolete by his science. Far from being condescending, however, he took his theological interlocutors seriously and remained courteous toward those repelled by his ideas. He understood their objections and empathized with their misgivings. Unlike the sophomoric putdowns of religious faith by some prominent contemporary evolutionists, Darwin remained remarkably patient and charitable in his treatment of those who resisted his ideas for religious reasons.

Perhaps this forbearance was due in some measure to Darwin's exceptional sensitivity to the pain of all living beings, not excluding his fellow humans. The long history of life's struggle, violence, and bloodletting that his discoveries laid bare bothered him deeply and intensified his personal sympathy with any organisms that suffer. It is all the more poignant then that the troubling idea of natural selection would become central in the mind of so sensitive a man. Yet if Darwin himself had not delivered the shocking news about the inelegant origin of diverse species, others would have. Even while he was still laboring to find a way to tell his new story of life without making too much of a theological stir, his younger contemporary Alfred Russel Wallace had already cranked out a nearly identical theory on the basis of evidence gathered during his own travels to the tropics. Sooner or later, scientists would have stumbled across the evolutionary passageway of life, and Christians would have had to deal with it.

Although many Christians still try to escape or ignore Darwin's message, his revolutionary and ragged vision of life will eventually have to be taken into account in any realistic theological understanding of God, the natural world, life, human identity, morality, sin, death, redemption, and the meaning of our lives. The question, then, is not how to justify Darwin's inclusion in a theological colloquy, but how one could ever justify leaving him out.

I doubt that anything makes religious thought more irrelevant, and even repugnant, to scientifically educated people today than the deliberate avoidance or rejection of evolutionary biology, or for that matter any other discoveries of science. After all, why should theology be considered immune to radical transformation in the light of new discoveries? Other disciplines such as geology, cosmology, anthropology, psychology, sociology, computer science, and medicine have already undergone a major retooling in the wake of Darwin's findings. Can theology realistically expect to escape a similar metamorphosis?

After Darwin, theology cannot plausibly be the same as before, any more than it could after Galileo. Nevertheless, a hefty percentage of Americans, possibly over half, still reject evolution. Parallel antievolution movements are gathering strength among Christians and Muslims elsewhere in the world. These groups repudiate human evolution in particular. Even seminaries and schools of theology seldom talk about Darwin and the animal ancestry of the human species in more than a passing way, if at all. Most Christian theologians still largely ignore evolution in spite of its potential to invigorate and profoundly renew their discipline. "Nothing in biology makes sense," says the famous geneticist Theodosius Dobzhansky, "except in the light of evolution."[3] Perhaps, as I shall suggest in the pages ahead, everything in theology also makes better sense when examined in the light of evolution.

In one way or another, Darwin has altered our understanding of almost everything that concerns theology. Most of the following chapters, therefore, consist of brief meditations on an aspect of life that Darwin's science requires theology to reconsider. Evolutionary science strains the meaning of almost every topic with which religious thought has traditionally been concerned. I list these relevant themes alliteratively as design, diversity, descent, drama, directionality, depth, death, duty, devotion, and, of course, deity. I devote a separate chapter to each. In doing so, I make no attempt to explore in detail Darwin's own interior religious journey. In spite of mountains of scholarly speculation, this territory is still somewhat of a mystery to us anyway, as it may have been to Darwin himself. Darwin's own life itself is surely an interesting area for theological reflection, and I shall touch on it briefly in the first chapter. But his theological significance lies less in his own religious ideas and doubts than in his new scientific way of looking at life. Nothing living or human now looks quite the same as it did before Darwin, and I intend to dwell primarily on the adjustments that Christian theology has to make if it hopes to stay in touch with the world of scientific discovery.

To accomplish such a task, in addition to reflecting on Darwin's own ideas, I include concurrent reference to several present-day evolutionists, especially Richard Dawkins and Daniel Dennett, who consider theology and evolution to be forever irreconcilable.[4] I do this for the simple reason that it is through their aggressively materialist interpretation of Darwin's ideas that countless people are now getting their understanding of evolution, along with the opinion that evolution inevitably entails atheism. I refer to their atheistic understanding of life as "evolutionary naturalism."

Dawkins is an Oxford scientist and best-selling author who claims that one cannot be an honest Darwinian and believe in God at the same time. It is hard to avoid at least some discussion of Dawkins in a book such as this, simply because his loud objections to theology in the name of Darwin have captivated so many readers. Dennett is a respected American philosopher who echoes Dawkins's views and packages them in verbose books, trying to show that Darwin's ideas have exposed religious faith as empty and theology as a vacuous and obsolete discipline. Darwin himself never came close to drawing such extreme conclusions from his own research, but Dawkins and Dennett have misled students, professors, and the public into thinking that Darwin was an enemy of all things theological. Dennett and Dawkins present themselves as inerrant representatives of Darwin, so I owe it to readers to raise questions about the accuracy of their radically antitheological reading of Darwin and his ideas.

Another proper name, that of a town and county in rural Pennsylvania, also tacitly shapes some of this book's theological reflections on Darwin. "Dover" has become a household name since 2004, when a majority of the members of its school board voted that students in the district's biology classes should be exposed to the anti-Darwinian set of ideas known as "intelligent design" (ID). This "theory," as it is misleadingly named, claims that the intricate design of eyes, brains, subcellular mechanisms, and other kinds of living complexity cannot be explained by natural causes, and that science itself needs to bring in the idea of a nonnatural "intelligent designer" to account for what seems so improbable. Most people instinctively connect this intelligent designer with the creator God of the Bible, and scientists rightly reject ID as a nonscientific idea. Alarmed at what they took to be the Dover School Board's assault on scientific method, some parents in the district brought suit against the board over the constitutionality of teaching ID as an "alternative" to biological evolution in public schools. They won their case. Since I testified on behalf of the plaintiffs at the trial, I call upon my experience there as I consider some of the present-day religious reactions to Darwin's writings.

Rather than approaching the topic of Darwin and theology in a historical fashion, in these pages I concentrate on specific concepts—such as design, descent, and diversity—whose theological interpretation must now undergo drastic revision in the light of evolution. Christian theology, I firmly believe, cannot responsibly take refuge in pre-Darwinian understandings of these concepts. Instead, it must look for theological reflection broad enough to assimilate all that is new in scientific research without in any way abandoning the substance of Christian teaching. This theological task requires a deep respect for traditional creeds and biblical texts, but it also assumes that in the light of new experience and scientific research, constant reinterpretation of fundamental beliefs is essential to keep any religion alive and honest. This is especially the case with Christianity after Darwin.

Meanwhile, Darwinian science also continues to evolve. Biologists are still learning more about how evolution works. They are gathering molecular, cellular, genetic, ethological, and ecological information about life, information that Darwin himself could never have known about. Nevertheless, Darwin's work has already raised the main questions for theology that still arise today. I am confident that any future developments in biology will bring up essentially the same theological issues that Darwin's own works pushed to the surface a century and a half ago. Many years from now questions about the meaning of design, diversity, descent, and other topics treated in this book will be as theologically alive and interesting as they are today.

The seeming artificiality of my alliterative—and perhaps mnemonically helpful—chapter headings should not obscure what I hope will be a substantive treatment of the startling questions that Darwin first raised for Christian faith and theology in the nineteenth century and that continue into the twenty-first. Not every ramification can be covered in each chapter, and the topic on which each chapter dwells is inseparable from those topics treated in the other chapters. My hope, however, is that by the end of the book, readers will have been provided with at least some of the ingredients for a contemporary theology of evolution.

Chapter 1

Darwin

I had no intention to write atheistically. . . . I can see no reason, why a man, or other animal, may not have been aboriginally produced by other laws; & that all these laws may have been expressly designed by an omniscient creator, who foresaw every future event & consequence. But the more I think the more bewildered I become.
—*Charles Darwin, "Letter to the Harvard botanist Asa Gray," May 1860*

Formerly I was led . . . to the firm conviction of the existence of God, and of the immortality of the soul. In my Journal I wrote that whilst standing in the midst of the grandeur of a Brazilian forest: "It is not possible to give an adequate idea of the higher feelings of wonder, admiration, and devotion, which fill and elevate the mind." I well remember my conviction that there is more in man than the mere breath of his body. But now the grandest scenes would not cause any such convictions and feelings to rise in my mind.
—*Charles Darwin in 1870*[1]

At the youthful age of twenty-two, Charles Darwin began his famous five-year sea voyage (1831–36). It turned out to be one of the most important travel adventures anyone on earth has ever undertaken. Our world has not been the same since. Even those millions of people who refuse to accept what Darwin discovered still feel the impact of his work. You would not be reading this book unless his writings had given rise to important theological controversies. You would not be wondering, along with me, what difference Darwin makes when it comes to such important questions as who we are, where we came from, where we are going, and what we should be doing with our lives.

Darwin's breakthrough book was originally titled *On the Origin of Species by Means of Natural Selection, or the Preservation of Favoured Races in the Struggle for Life*. First published in 1859, by the time the sixth edition arrived the title had been mercifully elided. I shall be citing this latest edition (1872) and referring to it simply as the *Origin of Species*.

Darwin's masterpiece launched an intellectual and cultural revolution more sensational than any since Galileo. The revolution is not over. The discovery that the earth is a planet moving around the sun was disturbing enough when common people, philosophers, and popes first heard about it. Galileo's sun-centered cosmology destroyed the ageless belief that the superlunary world is fixed in unchanging perfection. "'Tis all in pieces, all coherence gone," the poet John Donne had written about his impressions of nature in 1612, two years after Galileo had published science's first bestseller *The Starry Messenger*. But Galileo and the emerging scientific revolution did not lead Donne to question his Anglican creed, and the new cosmology caused few people to lose their faith in God. The same cannot be said of Darwin's new picture of life.

The *Origin of Species* sold out on the first day of publication, and with its appearance science entered a brand-new age. Not only did the biological sciences begin to undergo a dramatic transformation, but eventually other disciplines from anthropology to economics would also begin to follow the Darwinian drift. Nowadays the ideas forged at Down House, Darwin's home in the English countryside, are having more influence in the intellectual world than ever. What is most intriguing for theologians is that countless people think this influence includes a decisive debunking of religion. In the United States a good percentage of the religious population associates "Darwinism" with atheism, and many scientists and philosophers do too. Evolution, they say, makes the most sense if we assume that the universe is godless. After Darwin, as the renowned evolutionist Richard Dawkins exclaims, atheism rests on a more-solid intellectual foundation than ever before.

Darwin himself never came close to drawing such conclusions from his theory. In spite of his doubts about some Christian teachings, especially the ideas of hell and divine providence, he remained close to the Anglican Church in Down. He had his children baptized there and took a leadership role in some of its charitable missions. He was involved in the life of the church to the point of expressing annoyance at the laxity of several clerics assigned to the parish after the departure of his close friend the Reverend J. B. Innes. Innes was to say of Darwin in 1878:

> I have the pleasure of the intimate friendship of one of the very first Naturalists in Europe. He is a most accurate observer, and never states anything

as a fact which he has not most thoroughly investigated. He is a man of the most perfect moral character, and his scrupulous regard for the strictest truth is above that of almost all men I know. I am quite persuaded that if on any morning he met with a fact which would clearly contradict one of his cherished theories he would not let the sun set before he made it known. I never saw a word in his writings which was an attack on Religion. He follows his own course as a Naturalist and leaves Moses to take care of himself.[2]

The Theory

Eventually someone else would have let the evolutionary cat out of the bag, but let us give credit to Darwin. Other scientists had already begun to realize that nature, ranging from rocks to rodents, changes over time. Still, it was Darwin and Alfred Russel Wallace, a younger contemporary of Darwin, who first illuminated what had been called the "mystery of mysteries": the puzzle of how new species can emerge in natural history. Wallace should be given his due as a codiscoverer of natural selection, but in the present work the spotlight is on Darwin, the more famous and more theologically interesting of the two. The modest Wallace, who considered the *Origin of Species* to be as important in the history of science as the works of Isaac Newton, would not have objected to our centering on Darwin's work.

Darwin's scientific ideas about life's common descent, together with the mechanism of change that he called "natural selection," still make up the core of what has come to be called "evolutionary theory." But Darwin needed help to become as influential as he is today. His theory lacked a good explanation of how physical traits can be inherited, and it was only after he died that the science of genetics arrived to account for variation and heredity and thus rescue the theory. Already in Darwin's lifetime the Austrian monk Gregor Mendel had demonstrated that traits are passed on from one generation to the next in discrete units now called genes, but unfortunately Darwin knew nothing of Mendel's work. Eventually the discovery of genes would become an essential part of evolutionary theory, and the fruitful marriage of Darwinian theory with the science of genetics is now known as the "Modern Synthesis" or "neo-Darwinism."

Even without Darwin, we would all have heard about evolution by now, and this entirely new way of looking at life would possibly have made just as big a splash. However, a distinctively Darwinian seasoning still flavors the idea of evolution. The theory has never worked itself completely free of its originator's assumptions, just as Darwin himself never fully shed his own theological preoccupations. Contemporary interpretations of evolution still feel Darwin's personal touch, and the theological controversies that the *Origin of Species* stirred up in the nineteenth century continue to surround the most popular presentations of evolution today. In the Western world, at least, it is hard for anybody—atheist, agnostic, or theist—to think about evolution without also thinking about God. It should prove helpful, therefore, to trace the steps of the theory's gradual emergence in the life and mind of the man most renowned for its discovery. We shall see that along with the voyage of the *Beagle*, the ship that carried Darwin around the earth, there is an even more adventurous journey of one man's soul as it drifts slowly away from its frail theological moorings toward the shoals of agnosticism. It is especially the latter voyage that will interest theologians.

In the case of Darwin, the theologically interesting itinerary began in a life shaped by a traditionally Christian belief system, and in the end it came close to the quite modern creed known as *scientific naturalism*. This is the name Darwin's friend T. H. Huxley gave to the relatively new belief that, as far as science is concerned, nature is all there is and that the search for supernatural explanations is not part of scientific inquiry. Since so many other educated people over the last century and a half have made a similar pilgrimage from an unquestioning childhood faith in God to the new creed of scientific naturalism, it is instructive to watch how some of Darwin's own theological convictions, never very fervent to begin with, began to fall overboard and eventually vanish in the *Beagle*'s wake.

The Voyage

Charles Robert Darwin was born in Shrewsbury, England, on February 12, 1809, a birthday he shares with Abraham Lincoln. He died in Downe, England, on April 19, 1882, and was laid to rest in Westminster Abbey. His father, Robert, was a successful and wealthy physician whose financial resources would subsidize Charles throughout his lifetime. Robert's famous father, Erasmus Darwin (1731–1802), had already portrayed life in evolutionary terms, although it is doubtful that his views had much influence on Charles apart from vaguely suggesting the descent of later forms of life from earlier forms.

Charles's mother died when he was only eight, an event whose effect on his character must have been profound but which is hard to measure. Later, the death of his own daughter Annie at the age of ten would prove to be more of a factor in Charles's abandonment of the idea of a beneficent deity than would the idea of natural selection. As a youngster, Darwin's preferred pastime was collecting rocks, shells, coins, and insects, and this activity may have helped him cope with his grief, just as a determined return to scientific work would later blunt the pain he felt at the death of his daughter. At any rate, Charles's youthful delight in collecting things certainly helped to shape the exceptional observational talents that would eventually fit him for the life of a scientist.

When Charles was nine, his father enrolled him in a boarding school with his older brother Erasmus. Throughout his formal education, Charles could generally be described as an average student, both in drive and achievement. At the age of sixteen he followed his brother to Edinburgh University, after being persuaded by his father to prepare for the medical profession. However, this Edinburgh experiment was to prove unsuccessful. Charles found the academic lectures, at least those he bothered to attend at all, tediously dry. But it was his witnessing the unspeakable pain in surgeries performed on patients without anesthesia during medical demonstrations that turned him away from following in his father's footsteps. Overcome by the howls of agony in two such cases, one involving a child, he later wrote in his autobiography: "I rushed away before they were completed. Nor did I ever attend again, for hardly any inducement would have been strong enough to make me do so; this being long before the blessed days of chloroform." Then he adds: "The two cases fairly haunted me for many a long year."[3]

On a brighter note, during his brief stay at Edinburgh, Charles began to share the interests of several other young naturalists, and with them he thoroughly enjoyed scouring the Scottish countryside for specimens. During the same period he also befriended an expert taxidermist of African descent from whom he began to learn the technique of preserving the cadavers of birds and animals slaughtered for the sake of science. This know-how would later come in handy on his sea voyage when he had to prepare the remains of diverse species to send or take back to England for closer study.

Having failed at medicine, Charles accepted the advice of his disappointed father and enrolled in Cambridge University, where he remained from 1828 to 1831. The expectation was that Darwin might there prepare for holy orders. He had never been particularly devout, but this deficit of piety did not seem to bother either him or his father, who also had little interest in matters of religious faith. They both fancied that Charles could best indulge his naturalist propensities if he were ensconced in a parsonage somewhere in the countryside. Yet such a languid dream was not to become reality either. Circumstances were about to point the young Darwin in a direction that would change dramatically not only his own life but also the wider world of thought and culture.

During his period at Cambridge, Darwin studied the widely influential works of Archdeacon William Paley (1743–1805), including Paley's important book *Natural Theology* (1802). Paley was renowned for his "watchmaker" argument for God's existence. He had reasoned that the orderly and adaptive arrangements in living organisms, on the analogy of a watch's complexity, provide evidence of a designing deity. Impressed by Paley's logic and eye for detail, the young Darwin accepted the conventional observation that organisms are adapted exquisitely to their diverse environments. This remarkable fact, Darwin agreed at the time, could only be explained by reference to the existence of an eminently intelligent and benign creator. Later, however, Darwin's own discoveries would persuade him and many of his scientific and philosophical followers to replace Paley's theological explanation of design with a purely natural account of adaptation.

By his own admission, Darwin's formal studies at Cambridge could scarcely compete with his enthusiasm for riding, shooting small animals, and collecting beetles. Still, during the latter part of his Cambridge period, he won the patronage of two instructors, John Stevens Henslow and Adam Sedgwick, both of them clerics as well as scientists. Their own love of nature, along with their kindness and encouragement, aroused in the young Charles "a burning zeal to add even the most humble contribution to the noble structure of Natural Science."[4]

Eventually, after an intense period of cramming, Charles passed his exams quite handily and acquired a degree from Cambridge. At this juncture in his life, however, he was uncertain about his future, still pondering the possibility of ordination. Then an invitation arrived (by way of his instructor Henslow) from the highly esteemed Captain Robert Fitzroy for Charles to accompany him aboard HMS *Beagle* on what was originally intended to be a three-year journey to survey the coast of South America for commercial purposes. Fitzroy, an accomplished naturalist himself, was looking for a companion with similar interests to travel along and serve as a conversation partner, someone to help ease the maddening loneliness of an interminable sea excursion. Having overcome the initial objections of his father, Charles gratefully accepted Fitzroy's offer and, after exhaustive preparations, set sail in 1831 on what would turn out to be, not just a three-year cruise, but an arduous and endlessly fascinating five-year voyage around the globe. It was a passage that would give surprising new direction to Charles's own life and also provide information about nature that would agitate the religious and ethical sensibilities of many Christians and other people ever since.

Aboard the *Beagle*, Darwin had ample time, when he was not completely immobilized by seasickness, to read Charles Lyell's *Principles of Geology*.

Lyell recognized that over the course of time, the earth's geological features had changed significantly, but that the changes had occurred only gradually rather than simply by occasional upheavals. Previously geology had generally endorsed catastrophism, the belief that geological changes, such as the carving out of great canyons, had occurred abruptly rather than over long spans of time. To make room for a literal acceptance of the biblical account of Noah and his ark, as well as the assumed short age of the earth, geological catastrophists had attributed startling formations on the earth to occasional God-sent disasters such as floods and earthquakes.

Darwin, however, was convinced by Lyell's work that many geological features are the outcomes of long-drawn-out, gradual change. Reading Lyell's captivating work helped prepare Darwin's mind to theorize that the story of life on earth was also one of incremental change over a long period of time. Whenever the *Beagle* dropped anchor, as it did for extended periods during its voyage, Darwin would eagerly explore the countryside; among his many new discoveries, he found what he took to be reliable evidence of Lyell's uniformitarian theory. Increasingly his newly confirmed sense of geological gradualism would provide a firm foundation for his theory of the prolonged transformation of life on earth as well.

In the Galapagos Islands and at numerous other sites during his lengthy journey, Darwin kept meticulous notes on geological features, flora, fauna, and fossils in the many places he explored. All the while he kept sending back to England specimens and many pages recording his observations for other naturalists to ponder. Hence, it was during the *Beagle*'s voyage that his name began to become respected in scientific circles.

Among the many questions that Darwin and other naturalists who later studied his specimens began to ask was this: Why, as recorded most famously in his observations in the Galapagos archipelago, do small but distinct variations appear among geographically distributed species of birds and other animals? After returning home, Darwin's own earlier belief in the special divine creation of each distinct species gave way to a strong suspicion that the origin of different living species had occurred gradually, in a purely natural way. Specific differences, Darwin began to suppose, could be accounted for without divine special creation if there had been minute, geographically conditioned cumulative changes in living organisms over an immensely long time.

Eventually Darwin began to doubt that a wise and intelligent deity would be so fastidious as to fashion separately each minute variation in distinct species of finch, iguana, or tortoise in an initial act of creation. The young naturalist became increasingly convinced that Lyell was correct in surmising that habitats had changed gradually over the course of time. So it was not a great leap to suppose that life had adapted to these new habitats gradually as well. It is possible that even during the latter part of his travel on the *Beagle*, Darwin was already beginning to turn away from conventional Christianity's belief in special creation. At this time his theological sensibilities may have started to move, almost imperceptibly at first, toward a rather dispassionate agnosticism that would never reach the extreme of atheism.

Back Home

After returning to England, Darwin began to feel the need for a more settled style of life. In 1839 he married his cousin Emma Wedgwood, and in 1842 the couple moved from London to a home in Down (later known as Downe) in the nearby Kent countryside. Plagued by nearly constant illnesses for the remainder of his life, Darwin helped raise a large family but still found opportunities to engage in biological research and write prolifically until his death. Fortunate to have inherited ample income, he could spend most of his days at home. There, even amid almost constant physical and more than occasional mental suffering, he undertook meticulous experiments, produced volumes of very readable scientific publications, and wrote thousands of letters to friends and fellow scientists.

As early as 1838, Darwin was already outlining his famous theory of "transmutation," later named "evolution." More than twenty years before the actual publication of the *Origin of Species*, he had already laid out the core elements of his theory of "natural selection." One evening, after reading Thomas Malthus's popular book *An Essay on the Principle of Population* (1798), the thought occurred to Darwin that the restrictions on human population growth, on which Malthus was a recognized expert at the time, applied in some manner to the nonhuman world of living beings as well. Malthus had theorized that the growth in human numbers is limited by the amount of food and other resources available. Given these constraints, Malthus argued, a struggle for the relatively scarce amount of sustenance available has to take place, and unfortunately only a finite number of human beings can survive while others will lose out in the competition. The stronger will survive and the weak will be eliminated.

Darwin began to speculate, correspondingly, that a ruthless principle of selection and a similar "struggle for existence" have always been operative among members of all species of life. In this way natural selection could account for the gradual evolution and diversification of species over time. The "mystery of mysteries" would be solved. All organisms and species living today, he reasoned, have descended with modification from a common ancestor, and the various forms of life still extant could be accounted for by "natural selection." Natural selection is a mechanism by which nature "selects" the more adaptive organisms to survive and reproduce while eliminating nonadaptive organisms and even entire species over the course of time. Natural selection also explains how new species can come into existence periodically without special divine creation. Darwin would later supplement his theory of natural selection with that of "sexual selection."

In later chapters I shall have occasion to flesh out Darwin's idea of natural selection and its implications more fully. At present I simply want to point out how puzzling it is that after Darwin arrived at his theory, he waited another twenty years before publishing the *Origin of Species* in 1859. Only after learning that a nearly identical and well-researched interpretation of life by his younger contemporary Alfred Russel Wallace would soon appear was he finally persuaded to publish his own version. One might suppose that, as a good scientist, Darwin waited so long because he was simply being cautious, but he was also aware that several previous works by other writers on life's evolutionary descent had stirred up considerable debate and much hatred as well. So the postponement of publication may have been due, in part at least, to Darwin's reluctance to introduce ideas that he must have known would cause anguish to many religiously sensitive people, including his wife, Emma.

Pressured by friends, other scientists, and his publisher, however, Darwin finally agreed to publish his work. After appearing in print, the *Origin of Species* became an immediate sensation and deservedly so. Everything about life now looked different. In the following chapters, therefore, my objective is to dwell on the main theological questions about life that Darwin's work stirred up. I shall be dealing henceforth not so much with the historical person and preoccupations of Darwin the man, but mostly with what might be called the Darwinian specter, the set of ideas that he let loose and that, in scientifically updated form, continue to call for theological comment. I intend these compact reflections to be only starting points for the reader's own theological meditation on themes central both to Darwin and contemporary evolutionary biology.

Chapter 2

Design

Nothing at first can appear more difficult to believe than that the more complex organs and instincts have been perfected, not by means superior to . . . human reason, but by the accumulation of innumerable slight variations, each good for the individual possessor.
—*Charles Darwin,* The Origin of Species[1]

The old argument from design in nature, as given by Paley, which formerly seemed to me so conclusive, fails, now that the law of natural selection has been discovered. There seems to be no more design in the variability of organic beings and in the action of natural selection, than in the course which the wind blows.
—*Charles Darwin,* Autobiography[2]

Although Charles Darwin was a great scientist, his mind had been shaped, for better or worse, by theological concerns that he never fully got out of his system. From the time he was a young man, he remained personally preoccupied with a question that, during his lifetime, almost all educated people, including scientists, took to be distinctively theological. That question was how to explain the mysterious fact that living beings are exquisitely adapted to fit their particular environments. How remarkable it is, for example, that a fish's eyes, unlike those of most land animals, are adapted to seeing things clearly under water. The spherical shape of marine animals' lenses allows them to see things in an aqueous environment with a perceptive clarity that our own ellipsoid lenses do not permit. Why are the eyes of these animals so closely adapted to their environments?

Before Darwin's illuminating sea voyage, the favorite answer was "divine design." The young Darwin himself clung firmly to this belief, but later he arrived at a shockingly different answer. He called his new explanation "natural selection." It would imply that fish have spherical eyes today not because God directly designed them that way in the beginning, but because over the course of time they have proved to be more adaptive than the alternatives that lost out in the struggle for existence.

Later I shall say more about what adaptation and natural selection mean, but for now it is enough to observe that by introducing the idea of natural selection, Darwin was giving a new kind of answer to what had previously been taken to be a strictly *theological* question. He was now answering the question of adaptive design in a "naturalistic" rather than a theological way. Much of the controversy surrounding the name of Darwin still has to do with the fact that he appears to have wrested the whole issue of design out of the hands of theologians and placed it in those of scientists.

Does this mean, however, that no room remains for divine influence in the bringing about of such remarkable outcomes as the fish's eye, or for that matter, mammalian ears, eyes, and brains? To many scientific thinkers, it does, and no matter how you answer the question, it is hard to exaggerate the extent to which Darwin's naturalistic answer has transformed intellectual culture during the last century and a half. Surely Darwin was not trying to be theologically controversial in the *Origin of Species*, but there he was, an unassuming scientist, depositing a purely natural answer into an explanatory slot that had been occupied for centuries by no less an agency than God.

Replacing an omnipotent and infinitely wise creator with mindless natural selection is not something to be taken lightly. I seriously doubt that Darwin himself ever, with complete theological consistency, thought out what his substitution of natural causes for direct divine creation would really imply about life, human identity, morality, and culture. After all, he never completely abandoned the idea of a creator. He may have concluded that he had done away with the idea of a God who directly or "specially" creates design. By giving this job to natural selection, Darwin made special divine creation unnecessary, but this does not mean that he became an atheist. At the very least he let God hang around in the background. He still believed that God might be what theology calls the "primary cause" of everything in nature and that natural selection is a secondary cause.

Nonetheless, the way Darwin words things at times sounds as though the Creator has virtually nothing to do with evolutionary outcomes. Life's countless adaptive forms, Darwin says, have been produced *not* by a superior reason analogous to our own, *but instead* "by the accumulation of innumerable slight variations." Such wording can easily make it seem that Darwin leaves no role for divine creativity at all, at any level of causation. Certainly this is how Richard Dawkins, Daniel Dennett, and many other evolutionists have understood Darwin's work.

Darwin, however, announced his swapping of direct divine creation for natural selection in a soft voice and without any of the condescending swagger one finds in the evolutionist materialism of a Dawkins or Dennett. He took no delight in shocking the sensibilities of those who believe that God is the sovereign author of life, in all its splendor. Yet to many readers of the *Origin of Species* it has seemed that Darwin understood the term "creator" as a mere placeholder during all the prescientific centuries for what he was now calling "natural selection."

Christians in nineteenth-century England, the younger Darwin among them, had previously assumed that one could not account for adaptive design without invoking the notion of an almighty, wise, and good creator. But now, by allowing science itself to provide a new answer to a very old theological question, wasn't Darwin inventing a new kind of theology—at least in the sense of a new kind of *ultimate* explanation? If natural science can account for something as mysterious as the complexity of living organisms, including the adaptive fish's eye and eventually even the human brain, hasn't science now taken over theology's place in the task of making life's designs fully intelligible? And hasn't science thereby turned itself into a new kind of theology, or at least into a worldview that stands in competition with traditional theology?

This question is still quite alive. If natural selection is the ultimate and deepest cause of design, do classic theological explanations now matter at all? What good is theology if science itself can provide a satisfying answer to one of humanity's most burning questions? Isn't theology henceforth intellectually superfluous, impotent to make any sense of evolution?

An important key to understanding Darwin, especially in a conversation with theologians, is to look beneath the textual surface of his writings to find out what hidden questions are guiding his own search. I believe there are at least three such questions, each of them theologically laden, and that these form the subtext of the *Origin of Species*. The first has to do with living design, the second with life's diversity, and the third with life's descent. The present chapter deals with design, the next with diversity, and chapter 4 with descent. After briefly summarizing the theological concerns surrounding these three aspects of life, I shall propose (in chap. 5) that an appropriate engagement of theology with evolution can occur only after digging down beneath the themes of design, descent, and diversity to the underlying *drama* of life that Darwin's science has laid bare.

God, Darwin, and Design

The question of design was an important theological issue in nineteenth-century England, continental Europe, and America. This explains why Darwin, before his famous voyage, had been so taken in by the writings of William Paley. Paley was a highly skilled naturalist as well as an Anglican cleric; in his *Natural Theology* he had written that the intricate structural design of organisms is far beyond the power of nature alone to bring about, and that only a supernatural designer could have produced it. His famous argument can be paraphrased thus: Suppose you are walking in a field and you kick up a rock or lump of clay. You will find such objects unremarkable. But suppose also, as you continue your walk, that you suddenly come upon a watch lying on the ground. You pick it up and remove its back, exposing its amazingly intricate interior. The internal mechanism is so complex that you cannot fail to conclude that it was designed by an intelligent being, even though there is none in sight. Analogously, once you observe how intricately complex the organization of a living organ is—take our fish's eye, for example—a reasonable person cannot fail to conclude that it too is the outcome of deliberate design. What agency other than an infinitely wise, good, and powerful creator, though hidden from our field of vision, could have produced such a marvel?

As a divinity student at Cambridge, the young Darwin was dazzled by Paley's skill in observation and logical argumentation. Indeed, he would always admire the detailed way in which Paley described the complex design in a wide range of living forms. At first Darwin fully agreed with Paley that God alone could have created such stupendously complex structures as an insect's wings or the capacity of an organism to escape its predators. Eventually, however, Darwin would theorize that the selection and inheritance of tiny changes over the course of a long span of time could account for such marvels in a purely natural way. He did not rush headlong toward this naturalistic explanation, nor was it with great delight that he witnessed what he may have taken to be the collapse of the long and venerable tradition of natural theology as epitomized by Paley's argument. Nevertheless, one of the prominent developments in his intellectual and theological journey was a gradual loss of faith in divine design.

It is hard for us today to appreciate the gravity of this turn in Darwin's thinking. The drama that was occurring in his mind could hardly have brought him serenity. Toward the end of his five-year journey on HMS *Beagle*, he was already beginning to struggle with the question of how to account for design. He slowly came to suspect that the idea of direct divine design and special creation no longer made good sense; over the two decades immediately following his return to England, this tentative suspicion turned into hardened conviction. It is natural selection *rather than* special divine creativity, he came to believe, that accounts for life's design, diversity, and descent.

In his autobiography, Darwin reflects that his loss of faith in Christianity, which he had previously associated closely with belief in Paley's designer deity, was so gradual that it caused him little distress, but this is hard to take at face value. Within a solitary mind, over the course of just a few years, a purely natural account of living design was replacing a centuries-old theological habit of thought. One would have to be a lot more insensitive than Darwin not to have perceived how dramatic—and traumatic—this shift would be for many people of faith. Enlightened skepticism had been around for a while, certainly, but Darwin moved only hesitantly toward the rejection of direct divine design, and he was relatively tolerant toward dissenters to his theory. Unlike the in-your-face evolutionary atheism of our own times, his writing suggests that he was far from being fully comfortable with what he thought he had discovered.

Could such an epochal transition take place in the soul of someone so sympathetic with the suffering of others, as Darwin was, without causing any mental or physical turmoil? During and after his writing of the *Origin of Species*, Darwin experienced a variety of chronic physical ailments, including an almost constantly upset stomach. At times he could work for only two or three hours a day before collapsing on the sofa to relieve his fatigue, nausea, and headaches. Interestingly, whenever he interrupted his research and writing for a little relaxation, his health usually improved.

Darwin could not have been unaware that he was addressing a question that previously had seemed purely theological. His theory was not complementing but *replacing* centuries of naive theological opinion on divine special creation. Although in principle he still allowed God a distant role as primary cause, this theological adjustment must have done little to alleviate his realization that he was subverting a highly revered tradition of thought. As he began shaping his theory of natural selection, all around him even his most trusted friends, including such luminaries as Charles Lyell and Joseph Hooker, at first remained entrenched special creationists and continued to embrace the current natural theology's design argument for God's existence. Surely Darwin must have suspected that his notion of natural selection would be controversial even to the most open-minded readers of the *Origin of Species*.

Although his own account of living design turned out to be decidedly different from that of traditional natural theologians, Darwin no doubt understood that the question of how to explain design had arisen originally as a religious and theological concern. Religion and theology have appealed to people, after all, because they provide a haven of order in a world where chaos is a constant threat. The symbols, myths, and creeds of religion express a basic human trust that order will prevail over disorder and confusion, at least in the end. Nothing could be more attractive to most people than the promise of an ultimate victory of design over disarray, especially since our lives are hemmed in by the threats of death, disease, guilt, meaninglessness, and countless other sources of anxiety. So the religious appeal of Paley's focus on design in the nineteenth century, not unlike the allure of ID to many people today, is not terribly hard to understand. In an often chaotic and capricious world, and amid life's plentiful sorrows and inevitable perishing, instances of adaptive design stand out as emblems of ultimate coherence and as barricades against absurdity. For a religious person, the complex design in nature functions as a promise of the ultimate victory of order over disorder. Darwin could not have been totally innocent of all this or indifferent to it.

Today the fundamental reason so many Christians (and Muslims) are attracted to ID is that life's exceptional display of complex arrangements somehow makes it immediately evident to them that an infinite rationality or wisdom underlies the universe. You may attribute their preoccupation with design to poor science education, political conservatism, obsession with certitude, or faulty logic; but for ID devotees, design functions to hold bedlam at bay, much as Paley's natural theology did during the Victorian period. Surely Darwin realized that by dissociating adaptive design from divine agency, he was putting forth a set of ideas that most people, including himself, must have suspected of being theologically, and not just scientifically, revolutionary.

It does no justice to Darwin the man when present-day biographers suppose that he was only minimally bothered by the prospect that he might be opening the floodgates to an unprecedented torrent of religious anxiety. He was certainly aware of how disturbing Robert Chambers's widely known evolutionary treatise *The Vestiges of the Natural History of Creation* had already been to traditional Christians. And Chambers (1802–71) had not even brought up the idea of natural selection, the thorn that would prove to be the most theologically piercing in Darwin's theory. Darwin also must have realized that his own portrait of life, if accurate, would prove to be more explosive than the Copernican revolution. If so, one cannot wonder that trepidation would have overtaken him at times, and that it might manifest itself in physical symptoms.

One should avoid psychoanalyzing great minds from a distance, but it is hard to believe that Darwin could have been personally unaffected by the theological implications of his new theory. It is quite possible that some of his physical distress was the result of a disease he acquired in the tropics during his voyage on the *Beagle*. However, given his own sympathy for those in pain, the public agitation that he knew the *Origin of Species* would cause could scarcely have been such as to settle his nerves. It is no wonder that he did not rush to the publisher with his pages. It was only after Wallace, then in Southeast Asia, had sent him his own similar and independently constructed explanation of life's descent, diversity, and design that Darwin hurried to release his own more elaborately researched version. In doing so, he insisted on complete fairness by giving equal credit to Wallace as codiscoverer of the role of natural selection in life's evolution.

A Forced Option?

By 1859, twenty years after he had first come upon the idea of natural selection, it was time for Darwin to let the rest of the world look into his carefully guarded secret. The cautious middle-aged naturalist could never have predicted just how much anguish, controversy, and excitement his book would still be causing a century and a half after its publication.

It is hard, in any case, to look at the *Origin of Species* and not notice that something theological is going on throughout, at least in a subterranean way. Even while its author strives mightily to give the impression of wanting to be purely scientific, a lingering religious preoccupation festers beneath the surface. For years before publishing the *Origin of Species*, Darwin had slowly become convinced that it is natural selection *rather than* direct divine action that explains design. This conviction is usually interpreted as though Darwin made a clean break from centuries of theological ignorance and brought biology into the luminous new world of scientific inquiry. However, by placing natural selection in a competitive relationship with theology, however limited and unsophisticated this theology was in his own mind, Darwin demonstrated that he had not left theology behind after all. As long as he thought of natural selection as answering what was originally a theological question, he remained under the spell of the quite religiously tinted thought world his scientific mind was trying to shake off.

Likewise today, whenever evolutionists declare or imply that evolution is an *alternative* to traditional theological understanding, they are not yet doing pure science. They are still flopping around on the same plane of inquiry on which theology had been working for centuries. Even if they reject classic theological answers to the question of design, as they almost invariably do, they are still imprisoned by a kind of concern that is more theological than scientific. The evidence for this confusion emerges clearly whenever evolutionists insist that it is natural selection *rather than* divine action that provides the ultimate explanation of design. If they would stick to arguing that natural selection is an alternative to other proposed *scientific* explanations of design, biologists would remain safely outside the theological circle. But unfortunately, many Darwinians today, the chief being Dawkins and Dennett, do not stop with science. Instead they operate as cryptotheologians by insisting that natural selection is a substitute for the traditional theological accounts. They may think they are moving beyond theology; but by placing a scientific account in a place previously held by theology, they reveal that they too are still theologians at heart.

I cannot count the number of times I have heard or read prominent evolutionists and Darwinian scholars insist that it is natural selection *rather than* divine creativity that explains design. For example, Janet Browne, one of Darwin's best biographers, writes that after returning from his *Beagle* voyage in 1836, he came to believe "that living beings were *not created by divine fiat* [emphasis added]."[3] This kind of claim is typical of countless contemporary Darwinians. I doubt that Darwin himself ever intended to leave things at that. True, he placed natural selection in opposition to *special* divine creation, but in general his language did not formally exclude a deeper role for a "divine fiat," for God's creative "Let there be."

In contrast to Darwin's tentativeness, however, contemporary evolutionary naturalists leave no doubt about what they take to be the theological implications of evolution. Recall that in this book I am using the term "naturalism" as the belief that nature is all that exists, that there is no creator, cosmic purpose, or conscious life after death. Naturalism can have other meanings for other authors, but I am using it here in its atheistic sense. "Evolutionary naturalism," therefore, is the belief that living traits can be explained adequately and ultimately in evolutionary terms, and in a way that excludes theological explanation. My point, however, is that evolutionary naturalists (for example, Dawkins, Dennett, and others to be named later) are not leaving theology behind at all, even though they explicitly reject it. The ghost of theology still lives on in their hunger to find an *ultimate* (metaphysical) explanation of design in evolutionary biology alone.

Darwinians such as Dawkins and Dennett, for example, seem unaware that by using the expressions "alternative to," "instead of," and "rather than" they reveal their underlying assumption that evolutionary biology and theology are both trying to do the same thing: to provide an ultimate explanation of design. The difference is that to evolutionary naturalists, the idea of natural selection does a better job of it. They believe that in the quest to find a foundational understanding of design, science and religious faith are locked in a contest to the death. Theology and biology are rivals for explanatory primacy, and one of them has to lose. If it were not for the fact that they see biology as a substitute for theology, it would make no sense for Dawkins and Dennett to insist that a naturalistic account *rather than* a theological one has now come out first in the contest. By putting it this way, however, they simply show that they are still bewitched by theology. They are not yet doing pure science.

As a rule, competing parties have to be chasing the same goal in order for any observer to conclude meaningfully that this one rather than the other has won. It makes good sense, for example, to brag that your Pittsburgh Steelers rather than the Arizona Cardinals have won the Super Bowl, since both are playing the same game of professional football. But it would make no sense to say that the New York Yankees (a baseball team) has defeated the New England Patriots (a football team) since they are pursuing different goals and playing by different rules.

The lesson here should be obvious. If science and theology are supposed to be addressing entirely different sets of questions, it makes no sense to claim that one has defeated the other. And yet prominent Darwinian materialists are constantly preaching that natural selection has trumped theology in the design contest. Unfortunately, Darwin himself was sometimes careless on this point, and he never freed his science completely from theology either. But where Darwin was uncertain, Dawkins and Dennett leave no doubt about their secret theological obsession.

By trading in theology directly for science, many evolutionists today are also making another kind of blunder, the underside of the first. They are assuming that theology has for centuries been nothing more than a primitive attempt to do science in a prescientific age, and that it must now give way to a more reliable kind of science, especially Darwinian biology. Here again the fundamental assumption is that science and theology are playing the same game, trying to provide information about the natural world, and that modern science has proved to be much better at it than traditional theology. This false assumption, one that Dawkins shares with the literalist creationists he loathes, has been the dominant theme in his well-known fulminations against religion. However, by shoving Darwinian explanations into the same explanatory slot that theology had previously inhabited, Dawkins is still assigning evolutionary science the task of being a worldview or a whole new belief system. He is still playing his game in a theological arena, even if he insists that theologians must be disqualified from appearing there.

Consequently, we have to ask Darwinians exactly what game they want to play. Is it science or theology? Or is it both, as Richard Dawkins wants to do? As long as evolutionists claim that natural selection *rather than* divine creativity accounts for design, they are still trapped in a theological sphere of concern. They have not yet liberated science from the impossible burden of providing answers to essentially religious questions. They are not yet functioning as pure scientists, but instead as a peculiar new brand of metaphysician or theologian.

It is inconceivable to Dawkins that the coming into being of complex organic traits could be attributed in any way to divine creativity. When Darwin arrived at the notion of natural selection, he substituted it for *special divine creation*. He never denied that behind secondary causes such as natural selection there lies a more mysterious and less immediate kind of divine creativity. However, today's noisiest Darwinian atheists have taken Darwin's theologically unsophisticated phrasing to a new extreme. For them, when it comes to understanding life, natural selection has replaced divine creativity altogether and in every possible sense.

Since Darwin's time, meanwhile, creationists and ID proponents have been making the very same twofold misjudgment about design as Dawkins and other evolutionary materialists do. They too have been reading the *Origin of Species* as though it were intended to be the answer to a theological question about the ultimate source of design. They have interpreted evolutionary theory as though it were a challenger to theological accounts of design. For them, Darwin's science is an enemy that must be destroyed if divine truth is to survive. They have been looking at evolutionary science and theology as both competing for the same goal, that of providing an ultimate explanation of living design. The main difference between Dawkins on the one hand, and creationists and ID proponents on the other, is that in the search for ultimate explanation, each side arrives at an opposite verdict about the victor. Meanwhile, science and science education become the victims of metaphysical exploitation by both sides.

The Need for Methodological Modesty

Only after evolutionists come to realize that Darwinian science has no business in answering ultimate questions will biology be fully liberated from the clutches of theology. In many contemporary discussions of evolution, this liberation has yet to occur. Evolution can become a purely scientific theory only if its proponents give up the idea that it is a replacement of, or an alternative to, what had previously been theological explanations of design. Darwin never fully subscribed to this confusion, but Dawkins and Dennett have made it foundational to their thinking about life.

So also does Jerry Coyne, the latest loud voice on the growing list of evolutionists to claim publicly that Darwin's science entails atheism. A professor in the Department of Ecology and Evolution at the University of Chicago, Coyne has recently written a splendid introduction to evolutionary theory, *Why Evolution Is True*, a work that I enthusiastically recommend.[4] However, this otherwise instructive book is blemished throughout by Coyne's scarcely concealed theological obsession. Atheists, after all, have their own theological assumptions, and in Coyne's book we learn as much about his theology as we do about evolution. Like Dawkins and Dennett, he takes evolutionary theory to be the answer not only to good scientific questions but also to what had previously been an exclusively theological concern about the *ultimate* explanation of design in living beings. He is not content to present Darwin's theory of natural selection as an alternative to other purely scientific accounts of evolutionary outcomes—such as genetic drift or Stephen Jay Gould's emphasis on the accidents of natural history. Instead, he is mostly concerned to demonstrate that natural selection is an explanatory alternative to spurious theological accounts known as special creation and intelligent design. He does not seem to realize that by making advocates of special creation and intelligent design his main opponents, his otherwise excellent book is tacitly competing in a contest for theological rather than purely natural explanations. Coyne is still secretly obsessed with theology even in the act of rejecting it. Even though he rejects biblical literalism and ID, he places evolutionary theory in the same explanatory slot that these impoverished but incurably theological ideas had previously filled. As a result, what should be a purely scientific book is weighed down throughout by a theological heaviness that has nothing to do with biology itself.

In his new book Coyne tells his readers that accepting evolution will not turn them into atheists, but in recent articles and Internet offerings, he says just the opposite. He insists that theology simply cannot accommodate Darwin, or for that matter natural science in general. "One cannot be coherently religious and scientific at the same time," he declares.[5] He even chastises me and Kenneth Miller, a well-known biologist and Roman Catholic at Brown University who also vigorously opposes creationism and ID, for our shared belief that respectable theology can get along quite well with evolutionary science.[6] Coyne is troubled at what he calls my "accommodationist" theology of evolution. Why? Because the only kind of theology he wants to have a conversation with is that of special creation and ID. This will make things easier for him. Like the "new atheists" whom he emulates (Richard Dawkins, Daniel Dennett, Sam Harris, and Christopher Hitchens) he privileges creationism and ID as the normative expressions of Christian thought and is annoyed at what he condescendingly calls "liberal" theology for departing from the literalism that makes religion an easy target for evolutionist debunkers. However, by telling his readers what is and what is not acceptable theology, Coyne merely reveals all the more patently his secret obsession.

What I find most intriguing about Coyne, the outspoken atheist, is that he presents himself as an authority on what a "creator" should be like. Throughout his book he assumes an expertise in theology that is surprising for one who has obviously never studied it. For example, he is absolutely certain that if God exists, the life-world would display instances of perfect design rather than the imperfect adaptive experiments that evolutionary science reveals everywhere. "If organisms were designed by a beneficent creator," he charges, then we would never witness design flaws or "adaptations that benefit the species at the expense of the individual."[7] Such assuredness about the appropriate content of a deity's mind is remarkable for one who does not believe in God.

Obviously Coyne has acquired his theological learning primarily from reading and listening to creationists and ID advocates. For Coyne, antievolutionists represent the central core of Christian theology, as they do also for Dennett and Dawkins. Alternative theological perspectives that are comfortable with evolution are not worthy of consideration. So the more Coyne can make Miller and me appear to be like special creationists and ID proponents, the easier it will be for him to dispense with us as well. For example, he erroneously accuses me of inserting a teleological (purposive) dimension into evolutionary biology and of thinking of God, in the manner of special creationism and ID, as intervening miraculously in nature. I do nothing of the sort. Instead, I take pains, as I am doing in the present book, to let science be science, and simultaneously to let theology be theology. Scientific method, I have always insisted, should have nothing to say about purpose, values, or God's existence. It should stick to dealing with physical causes and avoid giving ultimate explanations. This way science can be liberated from the burden of providing ultimate explanations of the kind that theology has every obligation to ask about.

However, Coyne, along with Dennett and Dawkins, is unwilling to let science be science. He deposits the idea of natural selection in the same causal space that special creation formerly took up all by itself. Before making his substitution of natural selection for special creation, he fails, as Darwin also did, to sweep the place completely clean of all religious and metaphysical ghosts. He allows them to hover around so that they now attach themselves to his own unmistakably materialist creed. He thinks he is moving away from theology when he claims that "the great advance of Darwin's theory" is "to explain the appearance of design by a purely materialistic process—no deity required."[8] However, it is hard to find a more theologically loaded claim. Coyne is not only saying that "evolution is true" but also that "materialism is true." I would have no problem if Coyne were restrained enough to acknowledge that science must not even comment on, let alone decide, whether materialism is true or whether God exists. A methodological suspension of one's philosophical leanings and of any talk about God is good enough for science. But Coyne cannot help himself, and with every attempt to make natural selection a substitute for God, he digs himself deeper into the theological hole he shares with creationists and ID disciples.

For its part, theology can become reputable in an age of science only if it abandons any attempt to provide information of a scientific sort. It must allow that the Bible and other religious teachings cannot add anything to our store of scientific knowledge. However, scientists for their part must concede that evolutionary theory, or any other set of scientific ideas, cannot provide answers to religious or theological questions either. Coyne has not yet come to such a realization.

What Can Theology Contribute?

At this point many readers will no doubt ask, "Does theology have anything at all to contribute to our understanding of design?" The theologian must answer yes, but not in such a way as to give the impression of competing with or contradicting scientific explanations. To understand how theology may in some sense be explanatory of life and its wondrous designs without posing as an alternative to evolutionary accounts, one must first develop a taste for what I shall be calling "layered explanation." By layered explanation I mean simply that everything in our experience can be explained at multiple levels of understanding, in distinct and noncompeting ways. The idea that there can be a plurality of compatible explanations for a single event or phenomenon is an ancient one, endorsed by Socrates, Plato, Aristotle, Augustine, Aquinas, Kant, and many other great thinkers. They all embraced layered explanation, and I shall be arguing throughout this book that we may still do so in the age of science.

Layered explanation applies to almost anything. Take, for example, the book you are holding in your hands at this moment. How many ways can you understand and explain the existence of the page you are now reading? At how many levels of causation can you answer that question? There are many such levels, but to keep things simple, let's look at just three:

Explanatory Layer 1: This page exists because a printing press stamped letters in black ink on white paper.

Explanatory Layer 2: This page exists because an author is trying to get some ideas about evolution across to his readers.

Explanatory Layer 3: This page exists because a publisher invited the author to make a contribution about Darwin to its list of theological publications.

Notice that these are noncompeting explanations. It's not a matter of your being forced to accept one rather than another. You can logically accept all three without any conflict. You don't have to insist, for example, that the explanation of this page is the printing press *rather than* the author's objective of getting some ideas across, or vice versa. Likewise, you are not compelled to say that it is the publisher's invitation *rather than* a printing press that accounts for this page. All three layers (and more) are necessary, and they complement rather than contradict one another.

Analogously, Darwin and other scientists need not insist that it is natural selection rather than divine creativity that accounts for living design. Making such a claim is like saying that a printing press rather than the author's ideas is what brought this page into being. But in this case there is no need for any *rather than*. In a layered understanding of explanation, different levels of explanation are simultaneously operative without ruling one another out.

The "ultimate" explanation of this page lies at a deeper level than the printing press, and your discovery that a printing press has produced this page does not contradict the fact that this page exists "ultimately" because a publisher thought it would be a good idea to have a book on Darwin. Likewise, there is no evidence that just because natural selection accounts for the design of a fish's eye at one level of understanding, this excludes divine creativity as an ultimate explanation at a deeper level. What I mean by a "deeper level" I shall discuss later (in chap. 7), but right now I only want to make it clear that from an informed theological perspective, an evolutionary naturalist's declaration that "it is natural selection *rather than* God that explains design" is neither scientifically nor logically obvious. Such an assertion is parallel to the illogical claim that the page you are reading can be adequately explained by the chemistry of ink and paper *rather than* by the author's ideas or the publisher's initiative.

Let me explain. This page would not exist if it were not for the fact that a publisher has provided the enabling conditions for the author to put his ideas into words and for a printing press to stamp these words in black ink on white paper. Environing constraints or "boundary conditions" had to have been in place if this page was ever to make its appearance. Analogously, the various kinds of adaptive design that show up in the evolution of life would never have appeared if it were not for an enabling cosmic environment wide and resourceful enough to sponsor such a self-creative process as evolution and the emergence, by natural selection, of manifold forms of living complexity.

Asserting that this page exists because of a printing press and the chemical properties that allow black ink to bond with white paper is perfectly correct, but this account does not exclude the fact that deeper levels of explanation are at work as well. And it is important to add that these deeper influences—in my example the publisher's initiative and the author's efforts to express the implications of evolution—will never show up at the level of chemical analysis of this page. Yet this does not mean that these more-subtle levels of causation do not exist. If chemistry is as deep as you want to go in understanding this page, I have no objection, but then you will never even become aware of, let alone be interested in, the deeper levels of causation that brought this page into existence. On the other hand, a layered approach allows that a plurality of levels of explanation can lead you to a richer understanding, since each level leaves out causal factors that are operative at others.

Accordingly, the scientist's claim that natural selection "explains" adaptive design is correct, but that level of explanation does not take into account the fact that, for natural selection to work at all, there has to be a wider set of enabling cosmic conditions. As this book moves along, I shall observe that these enabling cosmic conditions include the fact that for natural selection to be effective, the universe has to have a generally narrative or dramatic character that allows evolutionary transformation of any kind to occur. Why this enabling narrative environment exists at all, and why it would favor the emergence of adaptive design by way of the "mechanism" of natural selection, are ultimately questions that allow a legitimate place for theological understanding, although at a different explanatory level, alongside, and not in conflict with, scientific accounts.

To return to my analogy—and no analogy is perfect—divine influence would stand in relationship to natural selection's production of adaptive design comparably to the way in which my publisher's desire to have a book on Darwin stands in respect to the working of the printing press that produced this page. The levels of causation are methodologically distinct in such a way that they cannot be smoothly mapped onto or reduced to one another. My publisher's intention will not show up at the level of your examination of the intricate mechanical structure and operation of the printing press. And you will find no "evidence" of my own objectives in writing this page, or of my publisher's intentions, while you are looking at the level of chemistry that bonds black ink to white paper.

Likewise, evolutionary biologists should not expect to see anything like divine influence intervening directly in the life-process at the level where natural selection is operative. Nor should they smugly conclude that they have ruled out divine creativity as a valid theological idea just because they see no "evidence" of direct divine manipulation in the formation of subcellular or organic complexity. Dawkins and Coyne try to decide the whole question of God's existence by searching for ways in which a "beneficent creator" would have to intrude into biological mechanisms so as to produce more benign outcomes than natural selection permits. But here they are merely placing on display their predilection for bad theology, stooping as they do to the same level of inquiry as their creationist and ID adversaries.

They seem unaware that ever since Darwin's own time, many theologians have not considered it at all inconceivable that divine creativity, intentionality, and beneficence would be factors in bringing about the enabling cosmic conditions essential for natural selection to be effective in the transformation of life over an immense period of time. Actually, as I have argued in *God after Darwin* and elsewhere, and as I shall propose in this book once again, a properly Christian understanding of God even predicts the kind of life-world that evolutionary biology has discovered and described. The causal effectiveness of natural selection at one level of explanation is perfectly compatible with that of divine creativity operating at a deeper level. (Again, in chap. 7 I will explain what I mean by "deeper.")

The narrow idea of "special creation" is hard to reconcile with Darwin's theory as long as it is taken to be the answer to a purely *scientific* question about how to explain adaptive design. Science looks for physical causes, and so appealing to the idea of God in any form cannot be part of scientific method. As a scientist, Darwin had every reason to reject special creation, as do biologists today. But in the *Origin of Species*, as I have been saying, Darwin was not always thinking and writing in a purely scientific way. Nor are Dawkins and Coyne in their own works on evolution.

My main point, then, is that if both scientists and theologians could now get over playing the "rather than" game, in principle they could allow that the complex design in living beings is a consequence of *both* natural selection *and* divine authorship of life. The latter is not a scientific kind of explanation after all, so it must not be taken as an alternative or challenger to the idea of natural selection. Dawkins and Coyne, who model their theological presuppositions on creationism and ID, will insist that natural selection is indeed a "better alternative" than divine creativity as far as explaining adaptive design is concerned. But such a judgment is as nonsensical as claiming that the printing press is a "better alternative" than my publisher's intention when it comes to explaining this page. Throughout this book I shall emphasize that a plurality of explanatory levels is available, and that it is possible to locate theological explanation of living design in such a way that it poses no conflict whatsoever with evolutionary science.

Welcoming Darwin

In concluding the present chapter, however, I state once again how important a conversation between Darwin and theology is for our time. Theology has everything to gain and nothing to lose by inviting Darwin to the theological conference table. We can be sure that Darwin's immediate response will be to decline such an invitation with the excuse that theological questions are too large for the limited human mind. "A dog," he would reply, "may as well speculate on the mind of Newton." However, by not fully forsaking his residual religious search for ultimate explanations, as we have just seen, Darwin has already invited himself, along with many other evolutionary thinkers, into a theological conversation anyway.

In the exchange that takes place, the first order of business will be for all parties to come clean on what theology is and what science is. Responsible scientists will agree that it is not the job of science to answer theological questions, and good theologians will rightly point out that it is not the task of theology to provide scientific information. After making these necessary distinctions, however, the dialogue of theology with Darwin is not over. As the rest of this book will demonstrate, it is just getting started.

Chapter 3

Diversity

Be fruitful and multiply.

—*Genesis 1:28*

Multiply, vary, let the strongest live and the weakest die.
—*Charles Darwin,* The Origin of Species[1]

Our ignorance of the laws of variation is profound. Not in one case out of a hundred can we pretend to assign any reason why this or that part has varied.
—*Charles Darwin,* The Origin of Species[2]

*A*long with the question of design, another persistent theological question was rattling around in Darwin's mind as he wrote the *Origin of Species*: How shall we account for life's staggering degree of diversity? Why are there so many different kinds of life and individual variations within kinds? The explanation of diversity had previously been not so much a scientific as a religious one. It is God's extravagantly generous creativity that underlies life's vast variety. However, by the time of Darwin, scientists were looking for nontheological accounts of variation and the diversity it causes. To naturalists in Darwin's day, the question was, How have new species of life replaced extinct ones as revealed by the fossil record? This is what the astronomer John Herschel (1792–1871) had called the "mystery of mysteries," and it was part of Darwin's mission to make scientific sense of it. Today much of the honor bestowed on Darwin is due to the fact that his evolutionary theory provides a natural explanation of life's immeasurable array of forms. Natural selection of accidentally adaptive organic traits over a great amount of time—this is enough, scientifically speaking, to explain life's splendid assortment of organisms.

However, once again, does this mean that theology no longer has anything important to say about life and its diversity? Do evolutionary explanations render theology utterly superfluous in this respect also, as Dawkins, Dennett, Coyne, and many other Darwinians claim?

People have always asked why there are so many seemingly distinct species of life. Creation stories from all over the world provide different religious answers to that question. Most Christians, for example, have believed for ages that God created each species separately in the beginning and that human beings were assigned the unique task of naming them. When Darwin began his sea voyage, he too was a "creationist." Like most other Christians at the time, he had no reason to doubt that all species had been specially created by God in their present form at the beginning of time.

However, as a result of his voyage and discoveries, Darwin gradually changed his mind. He came to assume that science should look for natural explanations of everything. It is not good form for "science," a still relatively new term in Darwin's day, ever to speak of God or fall back on theological explanations. Even some medieval philosophers had taught that the search for purely natural causes should be fully exhausted before appealing to theological explanations. And ever since Newton (1642–1727), many intellectuals, including theologians, had gradually come to agree that the physical sciences must explain the world without ever bringing in the idea of God. By Darwin's time the laws of physics were understood as operating reliably and autonomously without ever being interrupted or nudged along by any deity. Indeed, some early modern thinkers had already suspected that the notions of inertia and momentum leave little if any room for divine action in the inanimate world.

Still, living beings seem qualitatively different from the inanimate regions of nature, where the impersonal laws of physics reign supreme. Organisms are quite unlike nonliving things in that they seem to be driven by an invisible inner vital power. Endless variety and amazing degrees of complexity make life sharply different from rivers and rocks. So then, does the primary location of divine intimacy with creation perhaps lie in God's proximity to biological phenomena? Most scientists before Darwin still supposed that only a supernatural agency could fully account for life's standout qualities. But just as the domain of lifeless matter had gradually given way to purely natural explanation, after Darwin the living world was destined to do so as well. Today, Darwin's notion of natural selection seems to have demystified life completely. Living design and diversity have now been exposed as purely natural—or at least it would seem so. According to scientific naturalists, recent developments in molecular biology and biochemistry have finally exorcised the last traces of divinity from life and nature. Theology therefore is no longer relevant as an intellectually respectable explanation of life.

However, such an impression can be misleading. It is based not on science but on a failure to notice that science comes to know the natural world in a self-limiting way. According to the "layered" approach to explanation that I am advocating, scientific method is defined as much by what it leaves out as by what it includes. Methodologically speaking, scientific method deliberately blinds itself, for example, to what most of us consider the deepest and most important things going on in the world. By definition, science has to look at nature in such a way as to ignore values, meanings, subjective experience, aesthetic intensity, purpose, and the question of God. Even if God exists, science is not wired to pick up any signals of divine transcendence, nor could it express such awareness in a measurable way.

Science, one may even argue, is obliged to look at the observable world as if God does not exist. Theologically speaking, there is nothing wrong with science's doing so. Good theology even urges scientists to push purely natural explanations as far as they possibly can. Any respectable theology refuses to insert the idea of "God" into an explanatory slot where room still remains for natural explanations. To use the idea of God in such a way turns God into a "god of the gaps." To make God the answer to scientific questions is to shrivel what infinitely transcends nature into something small enough for mathematical equations to capture. This is bad theology as well as bad science.

So what relevance does the idea of God have in our attempts to understand life's diversity? If God is not the answer to scientific questions, then why talk about God at all? If even biodiversity can now be explained in evolutionary terms, what room is left for speaking of God, let alone referring to the deity as the infinitely gracious author of life? Hasn't science after Darwin demonstrated that such a revered idea now has no importance whatsoever?

Linnaeus and Darwin

Until not too long ago, the question of diversity had always been the occasion for religious wonder. Why does life fall into so many distinct kingdoms, phyla, classes, orders, families, genera, and species, of which there are millions? The Swedish scientist Carolus Linnaeus (1707–78) had already done an impressive job of placing plants and animals in different taxonomic groupings, but natural philosophers had always wondered how the distinct species are related to one another. As long as people could believe in special creation, the difference of one species from another could easily be attributed to a playfully ingenious divine originator. The countless species are related to one another simply in having a common origin in God's creative goodness and love of difference. Linnaeus's work, therefore, was a cause for theological celebration. By tracing life's diversity directly to the Creator's imaginative largesse, the Linnaean scheme could only enhance a believer's sense of God's providential concern for particularity.

However, hasn't evolutionary science now severed any bond between the variety in life and the supposed existence of a generous God? Isn't natural selection of chance variations a more elegant explanation of biological differences than theology could ever offer? Natural selection means that nature blindly selects for survival only those organisms that just happen accidentally to have the variations that allow them to survive and reproduce in their respective habitats. Why bring God into the picture at all? Isn't natural selection once again a "better alternative" than divine creativity?

Adopting an unhelpful expression from Herbert Spencer, Darwin often referred to natural selection as "the survival of the fittest." By "fitness," evolutionary science does not mean muscularity or physical superiority, but simply the probability an organism has of reproducing. It therefore is important to know what natural selection is not. Natural selection is not directly the source of the variety that appears in any living population. Random variations, which today are usually thought of as genetic mutations, are the immediate source of life's variety. The fact that one finch's beak is slightly better for crushing seeds than those of its siblings is simply a matter of blind chance. Natural selection "works" by allowing finches with the most adaptive beaks to survive and reproduce. Natural selection is not a conscious or intentional agency. Rather, it is a completely unconscious "filtering process" that discards nonadaptive organisms.

Curiously, even though natural selection is devoid of intelligence, Darwin sometimes bestows on it such a semblance of omniscience and omnipotence that it seems to have taken over the role that formerly belonged to the Creator. He writes in the *Origin of Species*: "It may metaphorically be said that natural selection is daily and hourly scrutinizing, throughout the world, the slightest variations; rejecting those that are bad, preserving and adding up all that are good; silently and insensibly working, *whenever and wherever opportunity offers*, at the improvement of each organic being in relation to its organic and inorganic conditions of life."[3] After writing the *Origin of Species*, Darwin sometimes thought that the expression "natural preservation" might be more suitable than "natural selection," but contemporary biologists prefer the latter.

Evolution by random variation and natural selection seems to be a heartless producer of life's diversity when compared to the biblical Creator's immediate warmth and love. In the first place, if an organism is to have traits that allow it to be "selected," to survive and reproduce, Darwin's theory implies that it has to be lucky. Sheer accident "rather than" divine intention or providential preference is the cause of the relatively few variations that nature will eventually select for survival and reproduction. When Darwin says that variations are accidental, he means that they are "undirected" by any intentional agency. They occur without any conscious consideration of their usefulness or survival value to the organism in question. Second, nature's selection of the lucky organisms occurs in complete blindness and with no sense of fairness, compassion, or justice, as far as individuals are concerned. Natural selection entails a "struggle for existence" among unequal organisms and species, and this contest causes considerable loss and pain. The unfairness and impersonality associated with natural selection seems to many evolutionists and creationists alike to contrast sharply with the infinite intelligence and beneficence that the Bible attributes to the Creator.

Third, in order for natural selection to bring about so many new species, an enormous period of time has to pass, indeed, many millions of years. Thus, at least according to human calendrical standards, by taking so much time, evolution looks inefficient and wasteful. Wouldn't an infinite wisdom, if it exists, do a more efficient job of engineering life's diversity? Furthermore, even with all the delay, death, and bloodshed that evolution entails, the varieties that survive are never impeccably engineered anyway. Adaptation is never perfect. So, isn't evolution proof that ultimately nature rests not on divine providence, but on an abyss of absurdity? How can one expect to make any theological sense of it at all?

Darwin's Theological Tendencies

Theologians might reply that God creates diversity *by way of* natural selection, but what kind of God would choose such a strange method of doing so? As the philosopher Philip Kitcher puts it: "A history of life dominated by natural selection is extremely hard to understand in providentialist terms." Pointing to the messiness of evolution, Kitcher observes that "there is nothing kindly or providential about any of this, and it seems breathtakingly wasteful and inefficient. Indeed if we imagine a human observer presiding over a miniaturized version of the whole show, peering down on his 'creation,' it is extremely hard to equip the face with a kindly expression."[4]

I shall address Kitcher's (not unusual) kind of complaint about natural selection starting in chapter 5. Here I only want to indicate once again that in spite of the apparent godlessness of evolutionary mechanisms, the shadow of theology still broods over Darwin's account of diversity just as it does over design whenever he takes natural selection to be an *alternative* to the traditional theological idea of divine creation. At times Darwin seems to be saying that natural selection is the *way* in which God creates many species, but at other times the thrust of his argument—and of much evolutionary understanding ever since—is that accidents plus natural selection plus time together constitute an *ultimate* explanation of life's variety, and that such an account leaves little or no explanatory space for theology.

Darwin's style of presentation, much as he tries to avoid it, still gives readers the impression that the incalculable array of distinct forms of life has been generated *not* by divine creativity, but *instead* by an unconscious, undirected, and unintended series of purely natural occurrences. As I observed in the previous chapter, the *Origin of Species* places natural selection in the same explanatory slot that had previously been occupied by the theological notion of special divine creation. Darwin had every reason to expel the latter notion from the discourse of natural science. Yet in an unconscious way, he and many of his followers, such as Kitcher, have situated another omnipotent and omniscient agency of creation, that of natural selection, in a causal niche that theologians had carved out centuries earlier. Evolutionary naturalists suppose that they have moved away from theology altogether, but when they claim that Darwinian process *rather than* divine creation is the cause of the enormous range of living types, they are still expressing themselves in an idiom that is more characteristic of theology than of science. In keeping with centuries of religious understanding, they are still seeking an *ultimate* explanation of life's diversity.

Whether Darwin intended it or not, the shape and style of his long argument has often been interpreted in such a way that it fails to prevent a scientifically illuminating idea—that of evolution—from becoming the basis of a whole new belief system. In spite of his best intentions, Darwin's writing had a tendency to bestow on natural selection the same metaphysical primacy that had previously belonged to God. And as soon as he allowed natural selection to take over the task of ultimate explanation, it sounded to religious ears as though evolution had become a rival of theology rather than a purely scientific theory that could exist comfortably alongside, though distinct from, theology.

By giving this impression, and without meaning to be controversial, Darwin fired a shot that has provoked a century and a half of unnecessary "warfare" between evolutionists and religious believers. Again, Darwin tried hard to avoid any conflict between his science and theology. He was even appreciative of the theologians who assured him that his ideas are perfectly compatible with Christian belief. But he was not sufficiently skilled in theological dialectic to convince every reader of the *Origin of Species* that by rejecting special creation, he could still allow for divine creativity at a more fundamental layer of explanation than that at which natural science operates.

Whenever scientists put forth a new discovery or theory as an *improvement* on religious or theological accounts, they are still assuming that science and theology are both in the same business, that of answering ultimate metaphysical questions. They are implicitly turning science into something comparable to theology, but this is a role that science was never intended to play and one that it is not very good at in any case. Logically, it makes no sense to insist that evolution is *better than* theology unless theology is assumed (falsely) to be a source of scientific information, or unless science (again falsely) is taken to be in the business of giving ultimate explanations. Readers of the *Origin of Species*, therefore, should be asking whether Darwin is giving a purely scientific account of living diversity after all. I believe he was trying to do so and for the most part succeeded, but his wording is at times less than precise in its distinction of science from theology. On the other hand, contemporary evolutionary naturalists (for example, Dawkins, Dennett, Coyne, and Kitcher) don't even try to disguise their belief that science does a *better* job than theology in the search for ultimate explanation.

Science and Theology

By any acceptable definition, scientific method is not cut out to answer ultimate theological questions. Even though some of the earliest modern scientists—Isaac Newton and Robert Boyle, for example—mixed theology with their scientific writings, science has gradually come to limit itself to exploring only the natural, material, or efficient causes of things. It is no longer concerned with ultimate explanations, purposes, or intentions. It is not permitted to appeal to the idea of divine creation or infinite goodness at any point in its method of inquiry. Theology, on the other hand, by definition wants to know the *ultimate* reason why things are the way they are. Consequently, theology must never cease looking for deeper reasons than science can provide about why life on earth diversifies into so many groups, phyla, species, subspecies, and individuals. Natural selection of random variations is a good scientific answer to this question, but isn't it possible that both science and theology can jointly render intelligible the "mystery of mysteries" without being rivals?

Without in any way rejecting evolutionary theory, theology may plausibly claim that biodiversity exists ultimately because of an extravagant divine generosity that provides the enabling conditions that invite the universe to become as interesting, various, and hence beautiful as possible. In chapter 6 I shall develop this proposal further in terms of contemporary theology. Meanwhile, notice that long before Darwin's day, the theologian and philosopher Thomas Aquinas (1225–74), just to give one of many possible examples from classical theology, had already asked why God creates so many different kinds of beings. His answer was that God created diversity so that what is lacking in one thing in manifesting the divine infinity could be supplied by something else, and what is lacking in that by something else, and so on.[5] The infinite divine majesty can never be fully expressed in finite things, even by way of an endless plurality and variety of creatures. Certainly no single entity, image, gender, species, or variation could ever fully express what God is. However, a plurality and variety is more expressive of the divine prodigality than a bland uniformity of creatures could ever be.

More recently the twentieth-century theologian Paul Tillich has suggested that in thinking about divine creativity, Christians should expect an unrestrained, infinite love to overflow in an irrational display of "holy waste." Human reason, with its calculative narrowness, is embarrassed at the unreasonable abundance of nature. Of what use, we ask, are the monsters of the deep to which Yahweh points in his answer to Job? Or together with the disciples at Bethany, we wonder why Jesus allows the woman with the alabaster jar of oil to waste it on anointing him when it could be sold for the benefit of the poor (Mark 14:3–9). However, Tillich states, "there is no creativity, divine or human, without the holy waste which comes out of the creative abundance of the heart and does not ask 'What use is this?'" Our indictment of nature's excess in evolution, therefore, may stem as much from our lovelessness and rationalistic narrowness as from the allegedly lofty ethical heights we think we have reached. In the cross, however, Christians discover the image of a self-wasting God, and so we must not suppress in ourselves "the waste of self-surrender, the Spirit who trespasses all reason."[6]

Perhaps it is with the same spiritual expectation of holy waste that Christians should look at the wildness of variation and diversity in Darwin's disturbing picture of life. That there are so many accidental variations squandered in evolution may seem contrary to the rigid design standards of human reason, but so also does the wastefulness of the cross to which, as we shall see, theology must connect the profligacy and suffering of all of life. But my main question here asks: Is the Darwinian account of diversity a rival or "alternative" to such a theological interpretation? Is it evolution *rather than* God's generosity that accounts for life's diversity? Why can't it be both, each functioning at a different layer of explanation? Science was never intended to answer the really big questions that people ask, nor is theology supposed to provide scientific information. Science and theology occupy two distinct levels of understanding the world. They are both able to give us truth, and they are not opposed to each other as long as each remains aware of its own methodological limitations. Science must restrict itself to finding physical or natural causes, theology to looking for deeper and nonphysical explanations. Science is not concerned with value, purpose, or ultimate explanation, whereas theology is so concerned.

Thus it makes no sense to say that living diversity is caused by evolution *rather than* by divine generosity, or vice versa. By pointing to evolution as the cause of biodiversity, the scientist is offering a reasonable natural explanation, one that can be revised if new evidence warrants it, but this scientific explanation does not compete with, or replace, theological accounts. Unfortunately, however, evolutionary scientists such as Coyne and Dawkins, and philosophers such as Dennett and Kitcher, have increasingly acted like theologians by taking evolution to be the ultimate, final, or deepest possible explanation of life's diversity.

"Rather Than"?

It would not be too surprising, in any case, if Darwin experienced some gastric distress after becoming aware that he might be *substituting* natural causes for divine creation when it comes to explaining diversity. Even though he was deliberately doing away with the crude idea of special creation, he had no substantive theology of creation to fall back on that would still give God a significant role in explaining the characteristics of life. Because Darwin must have had some suspicion that he was replacing a theological vision with a naturalistic one, it is hard to believe that he could theorize altogether without anxiety. I realize that many interpreters think otherwise, but Darwin could hardly have suppressed the thought that he was bringing about what would have seemed to his contemporaries to be a seismic shift not just in science, but in intellectual and religious history as well. Perhaps it would be too much for any solitary thinker to be the main agent of such cultural and theological upheaval without experiencing some degree of agitation.

I suggest, however, that Darwin would not have had to worry so much if he had been satisfied that the *Origin of Species* is answering only a scientific set of questions and not theological ones as well. At times he comes close to saying so, but he did not do so consistently.

Today evolutionary naturalists reveal their own theological enthrallment even more transparently than Darwin did whenever they persist in claiming that evolution *rather than* divine creativity is the explanation of life's properties. In putting things this way, they are merely putting science in an explanatory space previously occupied by theology.

The phrase "rather than" may seem innocent enough, but the whole explosive debate about Darwin and religious faith revolves around those two words. "Rather than" means "instead of," and it entails what logicians call a forced option: you must choose either A or B, but not both. If you choose A, that rules out B, and vice versa. Both creationists and evolutionary naturalists present us with a forced option: It is either evolution or God that accounts for speciation, but not both. So make up your mind and stop waffling and flip-flopping!

In this book's introduction I mentioned that I was a witness for the plaintiffs in the 2005 Dover School Board trial in Pennsylvania. During the trial I noticed that the news media were also inclined to frame the issues surrounding ID as a forced option: "Is it God who accounts for diversity," they asked, "or is it *instead* natural selection?" A forced option between God and evolution also underlies the writings of Phillip Johnson and other ID proponents, just as it is one of the main features of Richard Dawkins's works. Dawkins, in league here with his creationist and ID opponents, tells us to choose between Darwin and God, between natural causes and divine action, between common descent and divine creation, between scientific and theological explanations of the diversity of species. It can't be both!

However, logic does not force us to choose between theological and evolutionary explanations of life's diversity. As with design, life's diversity allows for many levels of explanation. There is no good reason, therefore, to question God's extravagant creative generosity just because Darwin and other scientists have recently discovered an evolutionary understanding of biodiversity. To do so would be comparable to questioning the causal role of the author or publisher in explaining this page's existence after you have learned how chemical properties can bond black ink to white paper.

You don't have to dismiss the causal role of a publisher or author now that you have discovered that a printing press brought this page into being. Likewise, your discovery that natural causes were essential to the production of millions of different species over billions of years of evolution need not threaten your belief that the extravagant goodness of a divine creator is the ultimate reason for life's variety. Maybe God grants to nature itself the enabling conditions and resourcefulness to unfold spontaneously in an indeterminate range of kinds—without any divine micromanaging of the process. The "wasteful" creativity we see in the evolution of life is completely consistent with an infinite love that overflows with limitless goodness and respects the freedom and independence of the various creatures that such bountiful-ness lets loose.

Theologically speaking, divine creativity entails an exuberant liberation of life that miserly humans may consider excessive. Such munificence on God's part amounts to an extravagant "letting be" of life, but this letting be is not recklessness or abdication. God's involvement in the evolution of living diversity seems all the more intense precisely because God wants creatures to share uniquely in a wildly immoderate creative process. What I mean is that genuine love risks allowing plenty of room for the spontaneity of the beloved. As we know from our own interpersonal experience, people we cherish the most are precisely the ones who offer us extravagantly generous opportunities for self-expression and life-enhancement. We feel most blessed in the presence of those who indulge our excesses, and who in doing so do not force themselves upon us.

Analogously, a candid theological reflection on the idea of an unbounded divine love should anticipate that such unrestrained generosity would offer a surfeit of opportunities for variety as the world comes into being. An infinite love would not stamp fixed design directly onto the creation in a dictatorial way but would allow the world to experiment with a superabundant plurality of possibilities. This theological proposal may go a long way toward ulti-mately explaining why there would be so many accidents (such as genetic mutations) and so much "contingency" in natural history, and why natural selection is given scope to act so autonomously—even if ruthlessly—when we look at it from a purely human point of view. More on this later.

In closing this chapter, I want to emphasize again that if both scientists and theologians could become open to the idea of layered explanation, the phrase "rather than" would not show up as often as it does in contemporary discussions of faith and evolution. Neither science nor logic compels us to make an either/or choice. Life's design and diversity are the results of both evolution *and* divine creativity. The same is true of life's descent, as we shall now see.

Chapter 4

Descent

The innumerable species, genera and families, with which this world is peopled, are all descended, each within its own class or group, from common parents, and have all been modified in the course of descent.
—Charles Darwin, The Origin of Species[1]

At last I fell asleep on the grass & awoke with a chorus of birds singing around me, & squirrels running up the trees & some Woodpeckers laughing, & it was as pleasant a rural scene as ever I saw, & did not care one penny how any of the beasts or birds had been formed.
—from a letter by Charles Darwin to his wife, Emma[2]

I have gradually learnt to see that it is just as noble a conception of Deity, to believe that He created primal forms capable of self-development into all forms needful pro tempore and pro loco, as to believe that He required a fresh act of intervention to supply the lacunas which He Himself had made. I question whether the former be not the loftier thought.
—Anglican theologian Charles Kingsley
in a letter to Charles Darwin[3]

*B*y Darwin's time, the suspicion that all living beings have descended from a shared ancestry was already spreading among scientists and educated religious believers. Even Charles's grandfather Erasmus Darwin had proposed that life unfolds and diversifies gradually over a long stretch of time. Some scientists, philosophers, and theologians had already accepted the idea of common descent as consistent with Christian doctrine. According to traditional theology, the creativity of God is not limited to bringing the world and life into being in the beginning. Creation can take place in three ways. There

41

is *original* creation, but there are also *continuous* creation and *new* creation. Continuous creation means that God gives ongoing existence to the world, and new creation, which traditionally points toward the re-creation of the world at the end of time, also implies that unprecedented forms of being may keep appearing in the course of natural history.

So the idea that nature can give birth to new kinds of being during the passage of time should never have been disturbing to Christians. The thought that the world can change dramatically, and that life in some way "evolves," is an ancient one. Augustine of Hippo (354–430) had proposed that unprecedented kinds of life come into being during the course of terrestrial time from "seed principles" (*semines rationales*) sown by the Creator in the beginning. Some contemporary "old-earth" creationists are willing to accept the scientific evidence that the earth has been around for several billion years, and they propose that new kinds of life have been created specially by God on certain occasions or at various intervals after the beginning. Most theologians agree with Darwin in rejecting this awkward idea of a series of special creations by God, but it is standard Christian theology nowadays to acknowledge that the creation of new being is still happening. God is not only the one who initially creates and subsequently sustains the world's existence but also the one who is "making all things new" (Isa. 42:9; Rev. 21:5). Since creation is not yet finished, considerable doctrinal space remains in theological tradition to accommodate the scientific evidence of descent with modification.

Ever since Darwin, consequently, scientifically enlightened Christians have seen no conflict whatsoever between the idea of common descent and the theological doctrine of continuous and new creation. Believers do not have to choose between evolutionary descent and God. Indeed, the idea of common descent as such need not imply any diminishment whatsoever in the power of God to create. Think of the Creator as bringing into being a world that can in turn give rise spontaneously to new life and lush diversity, and eventually to human beings. In that case, evolution is the unfolding of the world's original God-endowed resourcefulness. The divine maker of such a self-creative world is arguably much more impressive—hence worthier of human reverence and gratitude—than is a "designer" who molds and micromanages everything directly.

The point is not that God makes things but that "God makes things make themselves," as Charles Kingsley, Pierre Teilhard de Chardin, Frederick Temple, and other religious thinkers have put it. Theology has not usually been opposed to the belief that the creation itself can keep on creating in the mode of secondary causation. Even in Genesis, God says, "Let the *earth* bring forth living creatures after their kind: cattle and creeping things and beasts of the earth after their kind; and it was so" (Gen. 1:24 NASB). God is the primary cause, but God works through the lawfulness and spontaneity of nature. As I reported earlier, even Darwin at times referred to the classic theological distinction between a primary creative cause and a set of secondary causes that he identified with the workings of nature, especially natural selection.

In Darwin's books and letters, however, the idea of God as primary cause seems distant and uninvolved in nature, having only a negligible effect on the unfolding of life. To most readers of the *Origin of Species*, Darwin's do-nothing God has seemed to differ little from no God at all. Darwin never thought of himself as an outright atheist, but his severance of God from any intimate providential relation to nature has undoubtedly contributed to the emergence today of what I have been calling evolutionary naturalism, the belief that evolutionary biology provides the ultimate explanation of every living being's characteristic tendencies and activities. Darwin's proposal that life has descended gradually from protoplasm to human beings without any direct divine guidance has been especially hard for countless Christians to swallow. On the other hand, the idea that God directly designs living complexity after the manner of an engineer or architect does not match up well with either evolutionary science or a nuanced theology. So what is theology to make of Darwin's idea of descent?

The apparently mindless modifications that occur in the slow descent of life do not seem to be direct acts of divine providence and wisdom, as Darwin pointed out to his favorite American advocate, the Harvard botanist Asa Gray. Nor, as Darwin replied in horror to Alfred Russel Wallace's misgivings about the applicability of natural selection to the creation of the human mind, does the recent appearance of the human species in evolution seem to require, as far as science is concerned, any exceptional divine intervention. Humanity has descended on an unbroken natural continuum from previous chapters in the story of life on earth. No absolutely decisive line of demarcation seems to exist between primates, hominids, and anatomically modern humans.

What could it possibly mean therefore to claim, in keeping with Christian tradition, that human beings are created in the image and likeness of God? If our species appeared only gradually out of an immensely long process of animal evolution, what credibility can we give to Jesus' words that we are "worth more than many sparrows" (Matt. 10:31 NIV)? The highly respected Anglican bishop "Soapy" Sam Wilberforce (1805–73), Darwin's most notorious ecclesiastical opponent, has expressed as well as anyone the religious disgust that many Christians even today feel when they listen to scientific talk about natural selection and human descent:

> Man's derived supremacy over the earth; man's power of articulate speech; man's gift of reason; man's free will and responsibility; man's fall and man's redemption; the incarnation of the Eternal Son; the indwelling of the Eternal Spirit,—all are equally and utterly irreconcilable with the degrading notion of the brute origin of him who was created in the image of God.[4]

Although Darwin does not dwell on the idea of human descent in the *Origin of Species*, the notion is clearly implied there, and in his later book *The Descent of Man* (1871) it becomes the main theme. The latter work clearly challenges the constant Christian belief in human uniqueness and dignity. If, as Darwin claims, no sharp dividing line separates our own species from others, are Christians justified in thinking of human beings as having a dignity that makes them stand out unmistakably from other forms of life? Furthermore, what would our moral lives be like, one might ask, if we ever took seriously the idea that no crisp discontinuity sets us apart from other species? Can we sincerely aspire to be good if Darwin is right and we are tied securely by nature to the domain of animals? What would a post-Darwinian understanding of ethics look like anyway?

In more contemporary biological terms, what would arouse us to be good if our genetic heritage links us to organisms dominated by instincts to aggression and selfishness? Furthermore, isn't our apparent altruism simply the expression of what biologists now call genetic determinism? I shall come back to the question of Darwin and the human sense of moral imperatives or "duty" in chapter 9, but at this point I want to look at the more fundamental question of human dignity. If human beings have descended in a continuous way from the simplest forms of life, and if we share so much of our genetic makeup with chimps (as much as 96 percent) and even bacteria, what can the biblical stories of Adam and Eve's special creation possibly mean? In what way, if at all, are human beings special?

Considering evolutionary biology, can we justify religious teachings about our differences from other species and about our nobility and heightened sense of obligation? Genesis acknowledges that human beings are part of a wider community of life, and this is especially significant ecologically. But in view of evolutionary science, how can we think of ourselves as in any sense morally and spiritually different from the rest of life, as the Bible and Christian tradition do, if at the same time we are tied tightly to an animal ancestry by our shared biological history?

Darwin, Discontinuity, and Dignity

Darwin, I have mentioned, was not the first scientist to view living species as the outcome of "common descent with modification." However, his depiction of the tree of life, in which all the diverse branches and twigs stem from a common trunk and root system, makes the idea more shocking than ever. His fluid picture of life washes out the abrupt lines of division that traditionally kept the species separate. Darwin melts down Linnaeus's frozen system of classifications into an uninterrupted stream of living experiments. "Are there any clear dividing lines at all," he wonders, "between and among species? Does the whole notion of distinct species even make any sense at all?" Today evolutionary biology presents life as an incessant river of genes, flowing continuously from one generation to another. And since this same continuum of genes, along with the proteins they configure, can be chemically subdivided into large molecules, and the latter into atomic units, the question now arises whether there is any clear distinction between life and lifeless matter, let alone between one species and another.

According to contemporary natural science, life's gradual descent from a common living ancestor links up with the larger cosmic story of the gradual emergence of different states of matter and energy over the last fourteen billion years. Life is part of a much longer step-by-step cosmic process in which increasingly elaborate forms of physical complexity have "emerged" slowly, though not without episodes of regression, out of a primeval simplicity. The entire cosmic process is one of "descent" with modification from a primordial plasmatic state that existed fourteen billion years ago, culminating recently in the appearance of human thought, ethical aspiration, and religious longing.

This picture of matter giving rise by small steps to life, then to mind, morality, religion, art, and culture, has not been easy for all Christians to embrace. The scientific picture of descent seems to dissolve any basis for setting human persons apart from the realm of animals and the mindless matter out of which life spontaneously sprang. If human beings arose only *gradually* from less complex, less conscious, and less morally motivated ancestors, then at what point did the line of descent that led to our species stop being animal? If our emergence was only by way of small changes over millions of years, where, if at all, did our human ancestors step across a line that let them become a distinct species?

The easiest way of responding to these questions is to fall back on the traditional belief in special creation and deny that evolution ever happened. But what if you accept evolution? One conventional catechetical answer has been that our bodies evolved like everything else, but that our immortal souls were infused in each of us directly by God. It is in our having separate souls that we bear the image and likeness of God. So whether our bodies evolved from a common ancestry shared by chimps and anatomically modern humans is completely irrelevant. Our human souls are what make us special.

I don't know what the reader's reaction to this "solution" is, but I have long thought there is something evasive, artificial, and theologically shallow about it. I agree that theology has the obligation to provide a firm foundation for a sense of human dignity, and I am not going to propose that Christian theology now drop the idea of the soul. Even though Christianity's sense of survival beyond death is expressed primarily as *bodily* resurrection, the notion of the soul has functioned to drive home the idea of our eternal significance in the eyes of God, no matter how imperfect each one of us is physically.

However, many peoples have attributed souls to animals as well as humans. The word "animal" itself comes from the Latin *anima*, which is often translated as "soul." Thus, evolutionary science provides theology with a challenge to look for alternative ways of affirming the special value of human life without denying our animal ancestry and the inherent value of other living beings. If we are to be honest about it, we now have to justify our worth in a way that is completely open to the abundant paleontological evidence for human evolution. Is the body/soul dualism implied by the customary theological anthropology the best we can do? Can't we still think of ourselves as created "in the image and likeness of God," even if there are no sharp evolutionary, genetic, chemical, or physical breaks between the human species and its nonhuman progenitors?

Linnaeus's system of classification, with its abrupt lines of distinction among species, could easily protect Homo sapiens from being confused with nonhuman kinds. But if evolution really happened, we must now take into account the undeniable continuity between human beings and the rest of life. Furthermore, we need to acknowledge our species' dependence here and now on the total complex web of life, ranging from the microorganisms that allow us to digest our food to the larger physical and biological systems that sustain us and whose disintegration would be the end of us as well as other species. In this age of microbiology, ecology, evolutionary biology, and genetics, can we have a realistic sense of a uniquely human dignity without artificially ripping ourselves out of the entire fabric of life into which, scientifically understood, we are so intricately entwined?

Traditional Christian theology, as everyone knows, has also had a powerful sense of human descent, but the descent of the soul has been pictured as moving vertically downward from God on high rather than emerging horizontally from an evolutionary past that only gradually changes into living and thinking tissue. According to the classic "principle of plenitude," every level in the traditional vertical hierarchy of being had to be filled with its own distinct type of being. Influenced by Plato and his many followers, Western theology has pictured human beings as generated by God from up above and then granted a special, eternally fixed station at a relatively high, but still subordinate, level in the hierarchically ordered cosmos. Hence, the goal of human life, as articulated in Bonaventure's theological classic *Itinerarium mentis in Deum* (*The Soul's Journey into God*), for example, is to travel back up the ladder of being to God "on high," from whom all beings have descended.

At the lowest level of the traditional scheme of descent are purely material beings such as rocks and liquids. Higher up are plants, then animals, then humans, angels, and finally God. As we look from the bottom to the top in this Great Chain of Being, the levels become increasingly more valuable, elusive, and mysterious. Matter is easy to grasp, life less so, consciousness only fuzzily, and God not at all. Believers can have a sense of being grasped by the divine mystery, but they cannot grasp it themselves. They can speak in symbolic terms about the God from whom all the lower levels of being descend, but they cannot know God with clarity. Symbolic and ritualistic modes of expression may draw people upward toward the divine, but beyond that they must remain silent about the origin and destiny of all being. That which is ultimate in being, truth, goodness, and beauty can comprehend us, but we cannot comprehend it.

According to this cosmic hierarchy each higher level in the graded scale of beings evades comprehension in terms that pertain to the levels beneath it. Knowing what goes on at the level of mere matter, for example, does not provide the competence to say anything significant about the slipperier level of life. This is because, as we make our way up the pecking order, each level of being participates more fully in the unspeakable divine mystery. It is participation in God's own being that grounds the value of everything. The relative degrees of worth in different levels of being are proportionate to the degree of their participation in God. Thus the higher dignity of humans is connected with the fact that our rationality and capacity to love or make promises— the soul, in other words—participates in and ideally reflects the divine more luminously than do "lower" forms of being.

Today, however, science seems to have flattened the traditional hierarchy, blurring the sharp lines between nonlife, life, humanity, and ultimate reality. In alliance with cosmology, physics, chemistry, geology, and other sciences, evolutionary biology has now demolished—or so it would seem—the vertical arrangement of levels that emanates from on high and allows for our own relatively high standing in the scheme of things. The higher echelons of the ancient hierarchy of being now appear to have been cobbled together from below by a blind experimental process of natural selection taking place over a vast period of time. It is now hard to tell where one level leaves off and another begins. And to the scientific naturalist, the highest level of all, that of God, seems to be a purely human invention designed to give people false comfort in a pointless universe.

Consequently, many contemporary scientists and philosophers interpret Darwin's *Origin of Species* and *Descent of Man* as having finally shattered the venerable classic hierarchy, leaving only a spotty trail of undifferentiated physical components and evolutionary episodes. And the new picture of life as reducible to matter has tempted more than a few scientists to adopt a philosophy of nature that early twentieth-century philosophers such as William James and Alfred North Whitehead aptly named "scientific materialism." Scientific materialism is the belief that physical reality, as made available to the natural sciences, is really all there is. So if materialism is true, and mindless matter is ultimate reality, then there is no reason to think that God exists or that the intuition of special human dignity has a timeless foundation.

Darwin's notes reveal that he too was tempted to materialism, even though he would never have publicly flaunted such a controversial worldview. "Oh you materialist," he once wrote to himself in the margins of his diary. He surely realized that his startling portrait of the horizontal descent of humanity by minute blind modifications from a purely material past would clash sharply with Christianity's classic picture of the soul's descent from above. Darwin must have known that a purely physicalist picture of human origins would seem irreconcilable with the hierarchical worldview that for centuries had provided the basis for people's sense of identity and self-worth. Compassionate man that he was, how could he not have felt a bit unsteady about having to be the bearer of such a fascinating but devastating bit of news?

Theology and Information

Whatever his own views on the topic may be, Darwin's notion of descent with modification invites Christian theologians today to consider whether it makes sense to embrace an uncompromising belief in human uniqueness and dignity without rejecting the scientifically demonstrable evidence for our evolutionary descent. Paleontology and genetics are providing an increasingly reliable record of the gradual transition of primates to hominids to modern humans over the last eight million years. It is evasive on the part of Christians and their theologians, therefore, to speak of human dignity these days while ignoring and even denying this evidence. It is a scandal, for example, that some Christian denominations still assume that educated people must accept a literalist understanding of the biblical accounts of Adam and Eve and original sin. And it is deplorable that there are still so many defenders of ID and creationism, both of which consider it essential to reject evolutionary biology in order to defend the notion of human dignity.

How then, after Darwin, may one still plausibly hold on to the traditional Christian conviction that some levels of being are more valuable than others? Is it logically possible simultaneously to embrace a hierarchical sense of values on the one hand, including those associated with human dignity, and on the other hand to embrace the horizontal picture of nature gradually evolving from matter to mind? If personal beings emerged only gradually out of mindless matter, can one still subscribe to belief in the special *sacredness* of human life? Can the classic hierarchy of values be saved in any sense without repudiating Darwin's science?

Before attempting a response, let us recognize that the term "hierarchy" comes from two Greek roots, *hier* = sacred, and *archē* = origin. Although the word now has ecclesiastical overtones, I am using it to point to the religious sense that the universe derives its being from what is sacred or divine. The question is whether one can plausibly combine a Darwinian account of human descent with the honored religious intuition that the various levels of being have a sacred origin and value. Common sense, moral goodness, legal procedure, and human sanity all rest on the assumption that some dimensions of reality are more valuable than others. To abandon hierarchical thinking altogether would not only run counter to the fundamental beliefs of the world's timeless wisdom traditions; it would also be contrary to reason. For even to claim that the universe is devoid of distinct grades of significance, paradoxically one has to attribute an exceptionally high degree of value—perhaps even a degree of sacredness—to one's own mind in its capacity to make such a judgment.

Forsaking hierarchical thinking altogether, as it turns out, even goes against the recent trend in the natural sciences to highlight the reality of emergent systems. Science itself is more aware than ever that simpler physical systems are nested within more complex wholes that come into being during the course of natural history. A dynamic hierarchical organization is pervasive throughout nature. Atoms are enfolded by molecules, molecules by cells, cells by organisms, organisms by ecosystems, and so on. Nature is an emergent rather than strictly vertical hierarchy, but it nonetheless is a hierarchy. The spirit of reductionism may still be alive, but consensus is growing that comprehensive wholes such as living organisms cannot be reduced to their elemental constituents without losing something significant in the translation.

In the case of living beings, one dimension that gets lost in simpleminded reductionism is the dimension of "information." Information means that more is going on in life and evolution than merely molecular or atomic activity. Comprehensive *organizational principles* inform the more elemental levels, and we may loosely assign the name "information" to these principles. Information is not reducible to matter and energy but it is no less natural. Information is not something "supernatural" even though it may seem so to crude materialists. Many great thinkers from Plato to Alfred North Whitehead have acknowledged that things cannot be definite or actual at all without being patterned or ordered by some formative principle. In current scientific usage, information is identified at various levels as the sets of principles that organize subordinate elements and routines into hierarchically distinct domains.

In coming to an awareness of the fact of information, modern science has bumped up against something distinct from the mechanical or material causes that had earlier fostered reductionist views of life and mind. According to the philosopher and scientist Michael Polanyi, the most obvious evidence of information's presence and effectiveness in nature lies in the DNA in the nucleus of any eukaryotic cell. At a very low (or abstract) level of analysis, the DNA molecule may seem to be "just chemistry," but at a higher (or deeper) level of understanding, the informational *arrangement* of chemical letters (A, T, C, and G) is the most remarkable feature of the cell. The *specific sequence* of letters in the genes of organisms is what determines whether the organism it codes is a vegetable, animal, or human being. The arrangement of letters (nucleotides) in DNA does not violate the laws of chemistry and their uniform operation; if you look at DNA from a purely chemical point of view, you will not even notice the informational content the atoms and molecules are carrying. However, at a deeper reading level, the informational arrangement of the distinct "letters" in DNA stands out as all-important. Without breaking any chemical or physical laws, the informational aspect of DNA allows the letters A, T, C, and G to function as a code carrying the hierarchically higher-level pattern that makes you a human being rather than an alligator or cabbage.

So your existence as a member of the human species—and as the unique individual you are—has to do not only with your evolutionary ancestry or your chemical makeup but also with the *specific sequence* of nucleotides in your DNA. It is the informational ordering of triadic configurations of the letters A, T, C, and G in the nucleus of your cells that makes your existence and identity discontinuous with carrots and chimps. Even though you remain continuous with them at the level of your evolutionary, atomic, molecular, and metabolic constitution, the specific informational arrangement embedded in your genes (segments of DNA) is what counts the most. Even if you and other members of your species descended continuously from a common living ancestor, and even if your genetic makeup differs quantitatively from that of chimps by only a small fraction, the informational difference is great enough to produce a biological and ontological distinctiveness. In the arena of information, you stand out as discontinuous with the rest of life.[5]

Again, this informational aspect is natural, and its effectiveness in making living beings and species distinct is not a kind of miraculous divine intervention. Information is not an instance of "intelligent design," nor does it prove that you have a soul or that you are created in the image and likeness of God. It is beyond the capacity of science to reach such conclusions. However, acknowledging the importance of specific informational arrangements in the formation of individuals and species of life at least implies that science's recent discovery of the evolutionary continuity in life's descent is not enough to justify the claim that humans are in no sense special among mammals. The fact that we are informationally discontinuous with other kinds of life at least makes it conceivable that a theological affirmation of special human dignity poses no conflict with science. By the same token, the informational character resident in each of the other species of life, and the informational differences in the individuals within each species, allows that every living being has its own unique identity and value as well.

Darwin's portrait of life's descent may seem to destroy all remnants of the classic theological hierarchy, and this is why many religious people have either rejected evolution outright or refused to confront it head-on. Even many theologians have simply ignored evolution rather than look for ways to reconcile it with a realistic sense of human worth. What I am proposing here, however, is that an awareness of the informational dimension silently at work in the universe offers at least one way to understand how different levels of being and value can descend from earlier developments in evolution without being completely reducible to them.

These reflections still leave theologians with other relevant questions relating to descent, and I intend to touch on some of these in later chapters. My main proposal will be that our sense of dignity is inseparable from our capacity to open ourselves to the future. Theologically, I want to connect our sense of self-worth and the place of humanity within the universe to the biblical idea of a God of promise. The fundamental biblical theme of promise encourages theology to think of God as creating the universe and shepherding life's evolution—without coercion—by inviting the entire universe toward an ever-new future within the timeless milieu of God's unbounded, compassionate love. The God of evolution is none other than the God who calls Abraham into a refreshingly new future. I suggest, however, that in leaning toward its ultimate future in God, the entire cosmos is already ennobled here and now. Likewise, the process of life's evolution and the story of human existence on earth are infused with special value here and now by virtue of their being open to being taken into the everlasting embrace of the God who may be thought of as the world's Absolute Future.[6] At least in some measure, our own special significance or value consists of our inherent openness to the "power of the future" that goes by the name God.[7] We are not defined exclusively by our evolutionary past but also by the future toward which we are called.

As understood from a biblical perspective, nature is even now pervaded, in all its deficiencies and ambiguities, by God's promise. Its openness to God's future gives the universe a special status at each stage of its coming into being. But it is especially in the newly emergent human capacity to hope, to open our souls widely to the coming (*adventus*) of God from out of the future, that our own value finds a firm foundation and our sense of self-worth becomes most palpable. We feel most significant and most alive when we allow ourselves to be carried away on the wings of hope. On the other hand, whenever we give in to the cosmic pessimism entailed by evolutionary naturalism, our sense of self-worth declines. Defining ourselves solely in terms of the evolutionary past from which we have emerged, while failing to acknowledge the open future toward which we, along with the whole of life and the universe, are summoned—that is to ignore the very ground of our nobility.

Telling the evolutionary story of human emergence from a lifeless and mindless past is scientifically illuminating; yet the closer we identify ourselves with the cosmic past, or with the elemental constituents to which analytical science reduces life and mind, the more a sense of our true value gets lost. Yes, we are products of physical, chemical, and evolutionary processes. Darwin's portrait of horizontal evolutionary human descent is scientifically sound: at the explanatory levels of biology, geology, and paleontology, this is all that needs to be said. But other layers of understanding the natural world are also available. Without diminishing or denying the results of scientific research, a theology of evolution locates the whole drama of life and the entire cosmic process within a vision of a universe still open to becoming more deeply infused with being, goodness, and beauty as it is drawn toward its Absolute Future. Within this biblical setting our special human status and value, as well as the meaning of what it is to have a soul, must have something to do with our capacity to be grasped, renewed, and dignified by the inexhaustible Future we call by the name God. I shall develop these ideas more explicitly in chapter 11.

Chapter 5

Drama

> *Often [Darwin] worried about the sheer magnitude, the philosophical*
> *effrontery, of what he was proposing. He was rewriting the greatest story*
> *ever told, offering his contemporaries another Eden, a secular testament*
> *for the times. The tension partly expressed itself in his health.*
>
> —*Janet Browne*[1]

*E*volution means that life has the character not only of design, diversity, and descent, but also of *drama.* What makes the *Origin of Species* a compelling read is that beneath all its elaborate and often tedious scientific detail, it tells the story of a long struggle accompanied by risk, adventure, tragedy, and by what Darwin called "grandeur." A Christian theology of evolution locates this drama within the very heart of God. The becoming of the universe, including the emergence and evolution of life, are woven everlastingly into the kingdom of heaven. Within the ultimate environment that Christians call Trinity, beneath the emblem of suffering that we call the cross, and in the radiance of Christ's resurrection—the evolution of life merges with the great epic of grace, promise, and liberation narrated in the Bible and codified by the doctrines of creation, incarnation, and redemption. Understood theologically, what is *really* going on in evolution is that the whole of creation, as anticipated by the incarnation and resurrection of Christ, is being transformed into the bodily abode of God. It is not in the design, diversity, and descent, but in the transformative drama of life, that theology finally makes its deepest contact with Darwin's science.

Ordinarily science does not focus formally on this dramatic level of evolution, but nothing in the scientific picture of life and the universe contradicts a theological sensitivity to the dramatic character of evolution. It is actually because of scientific discoveries that theology now realizes more clearly than ever that nature is not a fixed set of things suspended indefinitely in space, but a narrative unfolding in time. Although Darwin's scientific intent is to provide a superabundant amount of observational data in support of his theory of natural selection, the *Origin of Species* is also distinctive for laying out a majestic story. Distracted by the recording of minutiae that was Darwin's greatest talent, readers may fail to notice the narrative thread that weaves together the book's pages and chapters. However, if they look carefully beneath Darwin's account of life's design, diversity, and descent, they will find that they are being drawn into the subtext of a compelling drama of creativity, loss, suffering, and promise that is especially congenial to theological comment.

This deeper drama—not the themes of design, diversity, and descent taken alone—needs to be the *main* focus of a theology of evolution. I propose that most of the religiously distressing issues associated with natural selection can achieve a theologically satisfying resolution once we recognize them as essential to the dramatic character of life and the cosmos as a whole.

Theologically speaking, the central point of interest is whether the Darwinian drama should be read as tragedy or comedy. Do all the countless moments of the life-story add up to absurdity and nothingness in the end? Or is there a direction to the story, and possibly even a redemptive climax yet to come, an outcome that might give a lasting meaning to it all? The present chapter looks at the dramatic character of life, and the following (chap. 6) asks about the drama's possible meaning or direction.

The Struggle for Existence

The story told by the *Origin of Species* is one in which organisms constantly face enormous odds against their surviving and flourishing. Darwin often speaks of living beings *struggling* to exist. Making an effort to exist seems to be an essential trait of all life. One way to distinguish between life and nonlife is to examine whether a being is capable, even minimally, of self-exertion. The nature of living beings is to strive and often to struggle. Whether it is a bacterium motoring toward a food supply, or a human being reading books in search of meaning and truth, all of life *endeavors* in one way or another. In more technical language, life is "conative" (from the Latin verb "to try"), and "to try" means to move from what is toward what might be. Life lies along the pathway between present actuality and future possibility. Even as it bears within it the causal past, life feeds on what is yet to come; when life becomes human, it does so especially by putting on the raiment of hope. Hope is essential to human life, and our vitality weakens in proportion to the ebbing of our capacity for expectation. But even before our appearance in evolution, life always had an anticipatory quality, a reaching toward new possibilities, a feeling its way forward that has now reached a critical juncture in the human capacity for hope or despair.

Since life and hope are both modes of striving, they are risky ventures. They have the quality of wager. For wherever there is striving, there is the possibility of failure as well as success. As the scientist and philosopher Michael Polanyi puts it, since life always strives, it operates according to the "logic of achievement." Living organisms have a capacity to achieve goals, but they can also fail to achieve them. No wonder the study of life is so interesting. Since living beings can fail, they are susceptible to tragedy as well as triumph. Unlike purely chemical processes that unfold unfeelingly and have nothing at stake, living entities risk the possibility of *not* realizing the goals they seek, however rudimentary these may be.[2]

Even the most elementary instances of metabolism put forth a kind of effort, as the philosopher Hans Jonas observes. The earliest forms of life generate membranes, for example, to keep from lapsing back into the inanimate world from which they struggle to differentiate themselves. In order for life to be alive at all, a resistance has to be overcome, but the effort to overcome also allows for failures. Life always means self-transcendence, a straining to go beyond, but such "going beyond" is inconceivable without the existence of limits that can be transcended only by "trying," and trying does not always culminate in success. Consequently, in life and evolution there is always at least some element of dramatic suspense.[3]

Such suspense is absent from purely physical processes. The molecules combining to form a crystal, for example, don't aim or strive, but simply subject themselves to timeless physical laws. It is true that living beings, like crystals, are made up of chemical elements, and one way to understand organisms is to break them down methodically into their physical constituents. But there is something about life that can be captured more accurately by the concept of drama than by that of dissection. As soon as life had burst forth in the universe, natural history made a break from the predictable routines of nonliving physical activity. With the first living organisms, a dramatic mode of being came into play. Tragedy then became possible since life may fail to hit its target. Could the same be true of evolution in general?

In a broader than biological sense, nature certainly has been dramatic since the very beginning of the universe, long before life actually emerged in terrestrial history. Recently astrophysics and cosmology have found in the preliving period of cosmic history an essential prelude to the story of life. Science has discovered, for example, that the forging of the atomic and molecular constituents of life in massive stars billions of years ago is an integral part of the life-story. Far from being merely stage preparation and rehearsal, the epochs of physical processes that occurred in the vast span of cosmic history before the actual appearance of life almost four billion years ago may be thought of as an overture to the opera. From the very start, the universe's physical constants and initial cosmic conditions had to be exactly suitable for life to exist and be the dramatic story that it is.

Whether the universe is dramatic because of divine intent or simply by accident is a question we need not try to answer at this point. For the moment it is sufficient just to acknowledge that after Darwin had turned our attention to the narrative character of life, other scientific discoveries have drawn the rest of nature into the drama. Now nothing in the universe lies completely outside the story of life. Moreover, even if there exists a large plurality of lifeless "universes" beyond this one—as some scientists speculate these days—such a quantitative immensity in no way lies utterly outside the story of life in our own universe. Even if a predominantly lifeless multiverse is only statistically essential to the existence of our life-bearing one, that extravagant totality is still narratively tied to the latter's existence. There is no escaping the dramatic character of the totality of physical reality.

It is perhaps his greatest contribution to theology that Darwin, almost without being conscious of it, brings out so palpably the storied disposition of life. And nowadays, due to developments in astrophysics, the story has become larger and more interesting than ever. Science now links the unfolding of life on earth to the entirety of cosmic history, and this widely narrative vista allows nature to take on a new kind of coherence. Just as geometry in the early modern period began to tie various cosmic entities closer together in space, these days the new scientific story of the universe links all events serially in time. Since Darwin's day, science has been increasingly revealing an irreversible dramatic story-line in nature that mathematical analysis had previously failed to notice. Science has now exposed nature as a drama that makes it more open than ever to theological investigation.

In the preceding chapters I have limited my discussion to separate theological inquiries into life's design, diversity, and descent, following the outline of most contemporary discussions of evolution. Up to this point I have left out what is most theologically tantalizing about life: the enveloping drama in which design, diversity, and descent are embedded. In this chapter, therefore, I begin probing deeper into the dramatic character of life as revealed by Darwin and subsequent science. Theologically speaking, I want to ask eventually, what is the drama all about?

Theology and the Drama of Life

As it turns out, the three components of Darwin's recipe for evolution—accidents, natural selection, and time—are instances of the elements essential to *any* dramatic story. Recall your own witnessing of a drama, whether a soap opera or Shakespeare's *Macbeth*. To hold your attention, it has to have (1) an openness to novelty or surprise, (2) a continuity or coherence that ties the stream of events together, and (3) a passage of time sufficient for the drama to unfold. A series of occurrences adds up to a drama only if it fuses unpredictability with some degree of predictability and a span of time ample enough for the relevant events to happen. This triplet of components is also the medium in which religions, myths, and theologies seek to make the world intelligible. All three elements—contingency, continuity, and time—are essential to any story, and they cannot be isolated from one another without splintering the narrative into disconnected droplets.

Christians who find evolution contrary to faith usually do so because they are focusing abstractly on design, diversity, or descent rather than the drama going on beneath the surface. The typically design-obsessed frame of mind with which so many devout Christians as well as staunch atheists have usually dealt with the question of God and evolution is a dead end. For theology, however, focusing on evolution as a still-unfinished drama rather than a factory of designs is crucial.

Unfortunately, contemporary evolutionary materialists have seized Darwin's rich story of life and bled the drama right out of it. Their mechanistic treatments separate the element of contingency in the life-story from that of predictability, destroying both suspense and coherence. Simultaneously, they turn life's temporal depth into a rambling series of meaningless moments leading to a final abyss. They typically refer to contingency as "chance," and to nature's lawful reliability as "necessity," both terms signaling for them the ultimate meaninglessness of evolution. Deep time becomes a battlefield on which chance and necessity fight a long and pointless war. Viewed in this fashion, evolution remains forever resistant to theological interpretation.

For example, the paleontologist Stephen Jay Gould claims that the ultimate source of life's design, diversity, and descent is the accumulation of "accidents" in natural history. This simple "explanation" of evolutionary innovation understandably makes it hard for Gould's readers to think of life as a story at all, let alone an important one. Meanwhile, Richard Dawkins instructs his readers that impersonal natural selection (the "blind watchmaker") and immense spans of time add up to a sufficient explanation of living phenomena. Dawkins's evolutionary materialism suppresses the possibility of real surprise in life, and hence of its drama. All evolutionary outcomes are the result of an impersonal, "pitilessly indifferent" set of physical causes. Both Gould and Dawkins, in different ways, divest life of its drama by resolving evolution into either blind chance or mindless necessity.

In reality, however, the three elements of contingency, predictability, and time merge inseparably into one another in making life essentially dramatic. In the concrete temporal flow of life, there are no mutually isolated compartments labeled "accidents" on the one hand and "inevitabilities" on the other. Chance and necessity are not mutually isolated sets of events. Scientists and philosophers label some events in nature as purely accidental and others as absolutely necessary, but the actual story of life cannot be dissected in such a way without killing it. Contingency, lawfulness, and time are inseparable aspects of the narrative cosmic matrix in which the drama of life unfolds.

Again, any attempt to make sense of evolution needs to focus on the drama more than on the design in the life-world. As I observed earlier, Darwinian materialists such as Dennett, Dawkins, and Coyne are no less obsessed with design than are the ID proponents themselves. Claiming that Darwin has disposed of William Paley's divine watchmaker, most atheistic evolutionists now assume that science has thereby scoured the last remaining traces of deity from the natural world. My point, however, is that the place to look for God is not in the design but in the drama of life. Along with ID devotees, Darwinian materialists suppress any sense of life's dramatic depth, a dimension of nature that is much more remarkable and theologically interesting than design could ever be. They have failed to notice that the very features of evolution (contingency, regularity, and immense temporal depth) that seem separately to rule out the existence of an intelligent divine designer still point jointly to something much more interesting theologically. It is the drama underlying evolution more than the ephemeral designs that appear fleetingly on the surface of life that most awakens theological interest.

Viewed from a dramatic perspective, Darwin's impact on religious thought is by no means as corrosive as design-obsessed scientists, philosophers, and creationists have assumed. Instead, the dramatic character of evolution is a wholesome stimulus to theology. The most important issue is not whether design points to deity but whether the drama of life is the carrier of meaning. According to rigid design standards, evolution appears to have stumbled aimlessly down multiple pathways, leading nowhere. But viewed dramatically, the apparent absence of perfect adaptive design at any present moment in life's long journey may simply mean that the story is not over and that we simply cannot make complete sense of it until it has fully played itself out.

If evolution has a meaning, it would be embedded in the narrative depths of life rather than in isolated instances of complex design that float occasionally to the surface. It is to the underlying story, not to isolated complex systems or elaborately structured molecular states, that we should look to make sense of evolution. But it is the nature of drama that it takes time to unfold, so that whatever meaning it carries cannot unveil itself fully to our intellectual curiosity or scientific observation at any present moment. So, if life is essentially a drama rather than a factory of designs, it is arrogant and shortsighted for anyone simply to declare it meaningless because of the imperfection of present and past evolutionary adaptations, as Dawkins and his followers do. In the midst of a still-unfolding drama, how could anyone confidently claim, here and now, to have a sufficient basis for such a verdict? What if the four billion years life has had so far, along with its multibillion-year cosmic preamble, turn out in the long run to be only the earlier chapters in an unimaginably extended production whose ending still remains far distant? Even if the physical universe itself is destined to perish in the remote future, its narrative essence, as I shall argue in chapter 8, can be thought of as everlastingly woven into the life of God and thereby endowed with permanent meaning.

Surely it is hard at the moment to stretch our minds toward such an eventuality, but the newly discovered narrative character of nature invites an adventurous theology to do so anyway. Such speculation need not be dismissed simply because we cannot make out any overall cosmic meaning clearly at present. How often, while watching a movie or play, have we given up in frustration at trying to piece together the seemingly disconnected fragments in its earliest acts or episodes? After failing to find any coherence in the initial movements of the drama, we may have dismissed the whole as meaningless. And yet, if we stuck with it, our premature vexation dissolved as the fuller unfolding of the work gathered up the early fragments into a surprising web of hitherto undisclosed connections. Likewise, if life in our universe is a drama, its present deficiencies in design may not be a sign of an overall senselessness but of narrative nuance instead. Indeed, if life were perfectly designed right now, as Dawkins's implicit theology demands, there could be no drama at all. Perfect design would mean that the work of life has been finalized. There would be no story but only stiff and static structures to talk about.

If life, along with the universe that bears it, is a drama, we can only *wait* for its possible meaning to emerge. Evolutionary naturalists, however, are impatient. Dawkins and his many followers have declared life to be manifestly godless simply because there is insufficient "evidence" in presently imperfect adaptations to warrant the claim that the universe makes sense. They rightly point out that present evolutionary adaptations are flawed, but

they fail to consider the possibility that the perfect design they are looking for would bring an abrupt end to the drama of life. They announce that
Darwin's recipe has now exposed "intelligent design" as not so intelligent
after all, and that therefore the universe has no underlying divine principle
of organization. However, they do not seem to grasp that what they mean
by design—perfectly engineered mechanisms—would be at home only in a
frozen rather than dramatically fluid world. Along with Christian antievolutionists, Darwinian materialists are so preoccupied with design that they fail
to feel the drama going on beneath their feet.

On the other hand, a theology of evolution wagers that the lifeless ideal
of design is too petite and pretty to capture the richer meaning of life. Life in
all its rawness is dramatic, and drama follows the logic of achievement, not
mathematical exactitude. Life is subject to failure as well as success, to tragedy as well as triumph. Sometimes it hits upon a survivable line of descent,
but in doing so it must try out innumerable itineraries, and in the process
it "wastes" an unimaginably long amount of time. Darwinians often comment that nature's way of inventing life is so inefficient that even the most
thickheaded human engineer could do a better job. However, what looks to
engineers like inefficiency looks to theology like dramatic suspense.

Moreover, the circuitous routes followed by evolution's dramatic creativity
may not be as unintelligent in the long run as they seem to those who think of
design along the lines of engineering and architectural criteria. Science writer
Chet Raymo makes this point nicely. He takes note of the fact, for example,
that the human digestive tract is so unwieldy in its "design" that one can only
be amazed that food can make its way from one end to the other at all. An
engineer, Raymo speculates, would make the digestive mechanism much
more elegant: "Roll that small intestine up into a nice neat coil. Straighten out
those kinks in the large intestine. Can you imagine the exhaust system of your
car in such a tangle?" Judging by an engineer's standards, the digestive system
is a failure. But is it therefore indicative of an underlying senselessness?

Consider likewise the twisted "design" of the human ear. Again from an
engineer's point of view, it too is needlessly convoluted. "Hammer, anvil and
stirrup: Where did those crazy little mechanisms come from? Five separate
membranes. And three fleshy loops that seem, on the face of it, superfluous."
Indeed, Raymo continues,

> much of the human body is an engineer's nightmare, showing little in the
> way of intelligent design: which is just what you'd expect if our bodies
> evolved by a process of incremental changes acted upon by natural selec-
> tion. The thing about evolution is this: Inevitably it moves toward ever

more finely adapted organisms, but the end is not foreordained and the journey is something of a drunken stagger.

Yet Raymo, not quite so obsessed with design as other evolutionary naturalists, adds the following:

> Now, before you accuse me of tossing an Intelligent Designer out of the picture, consider this: For all of the improvements an engineer might suggest for the human body, the body is still a thing that no engineer could hope to equal. Fabulously resilient. Capable of stunning feats of endurance. Exquisitely attuned to the environment. Agile, disease-repelling, self-repairing, purposeful, cunning.
>
> Evolution by natural selection, for all of its jerry-rigged solutions, for all its failed experiments and blind alleys, is a wonderfully efficient way to populate a universe with diverse and interesting creatures. If I were an Intelligent Designer, and I had a hundred billion galaxies (at least) to fill with wonders, I can think of no way more efficient to do it than by genetic variations and natural selection of self-reproducing organisms.
>
> You want intelligent design? Try evolution.[4]

A Deeper Coherence

Raymo is a religiously inquisitive evolutionary naturalist who now doubts the existence of a personal God. So when he speaks of "intelligent design," he is far from endorsing the views advocated by Michael Behe, William Dembski, and other ID defenders. Instead, he is drawing attention to what I am calling the dramatic makeup of evolution, and he seems to suggest that the drama is not devoid of a deeper coherence than the idea of design usually suggests. The dramatic character of life, he seems to realize, is not immediately transparent to minds preoccupied with design. Life's drama in turn invites the open-minded evolutionist to *wait* before making a final judgment about whether an overall meaning may be coming to expression in our still-emerging universe.

A theology of evolution, in any case, takes drama to be a much more exciting road to the discovery of God after Darwin than are analyses of fleeting and always imperfect instances of adaptive design. It allows that there is more than one way to bring coherence to events. Design is satisfying to those who think statically, spatially, and nonhistorically, but to those who welcome time's long reach and narrative nuance, design considered apart from drama is trivial. Contemporary ID proponents can take no comfort in Raymo's reference to a deeper kind of "intelligent design." Unlike ID proponents, Raymo embraces a fully Darwinian account of life. Nevertheless, the evolutionary theologian will be intrigued by Raymo's search for a deeper coherence in the evolutionary narrative than most other Darwinians are interested in excavating.

Can theology penetrate to a dimension of nature that lies deeper than design? Can it arrive at a region of being beneath the surface of life where religious faith and Darwinian biology may coexist comfortably? Ever since Darwin, in ways that most scientists have scarcely noticed, adventurous religious thinkers have sought a "deeper coherence" of faith and evolution beneath the "shallow coherence" of ID and other design-obsessed versions of theism. In the spirit of this generally ignored theological quest, I am proposing here that a scientifically informed theology will focus less on patently visible instances of design in nature than on the following question: Why is the natural world endowed with the exquisite blend of indeterminacy, lawfulness, and temporality, giving it the dramatic substructure that allows an evolutionary story to occur at all?

Digging beneath contemporary controversies carried on by evolutionary naturalists and their ID opponents, theology may seek contact with Darwin's science at a deeper level than either of the two opposing sides has reached. Scientists and philosophers who insist that Darwin has disposed of theology altogether have usually done so by embracing the same engineering and architectural ideal of design as their ID opponents. Clearly, if God is the author of life, they argue, nature should be more elegantly and skillfully designed than it is. Don't the adaptive imperfections and the general inefficiency of evolutionary outcomes prove that life was not intelligently designed after all? Far from opposing ID advocates on this point, Dawkins and other evolutionary naturalists agree with them that an intelligent deity would have to do a better job than human designers when it comes to manufacturing ears, eyes, and digestive systems. But since attempts at design in nature have been botched, God cannot possibly exist.

The science writer David Barash typifies this design-obsessed mind-set of most evolutionary atheists. Like Dawkins and Coyne, he begins with the assumption that theology stands or falls on the question of design. If God is the author of living design, he reasons, the design has to be *perfectly* engineered. All religious believers, he assumes, must attribute the intricate design in life directly to an intelligent designer, since in their view "only a designer could generate such complex, perfect wonders." Next, Barash goes on to point out that "in fact, the living world is shot through with imperfection." From there he reaches his conclusion: "Unless one wants to attribute either incompetence or sheer malevolence to such a designer [God], this imperfection—the manifold design flaws of life—points incontrovertibly to a natural, *rather than* [my emphasis] a divine, process, one in which living things were not created *de novo,* but evolved." It follows that Darwin's science has decisively destroyed any basis for theology.[5] We find in Barash, once again, an evolutionary naturalist trying to put religious ideas behind for good and who, in doing so, holds himself forth as an authority on the question of what is permitted to pass as acceptable theology.

However, Raymo's suggestions, as I implied above, point beyond Barash, Dawkins, Coyne, and ID—in a third direction. Raymo wants to avoid theology also, but unlike Barash, at least he is not fixated on the engineering ideal of "design." In principle, he allows for a deeper coherence or intelligibility in natural processes, a kind of narrative arrangement of life that transcends the triviality of engineering elegance or industrial efficiency. His reflections seem open to my proposal that the wild experiments of evolution, the inevitable imperfection of adaptations, and the crazy convolutions of eyes, ears, and digestive tracts are not necessarily incompatible with a deeper kind of (dramatic) wisdom at work in nature.

Neither Raymo nor Darwin would go as far as I am going here, but my point is that their ideas are at least logically open to theological understanding. A theology of evolution need not ignore the fact that life on earth, in all its waste and wildness, has actually brought about a far more interesting, inventive, and beautiful set of outcomes than ever could have occurred if nature had been put together from the beginning with no "design flaws," as Barash's stringent theological criteria require. Instead of a universe instantaneously ordered to fit Barash's and ID's stiff architectural standards, Darwin has laid open a world in which adaptive imperfections turn out to have been necessary portals to future creative results that flawless engineering could never have allowed to occur.

Darwin, in other words, has portrayed the life-story as a true adventure. Evolution is a risk-taking and extravagantly inventive drama. Alongside its lush creativity, there always exists the possibility of tragic outcomes, including abundant suffering and perpetual perishing. To Christians, there is something "cruciform" about the whole drama of life.[6] Sensitive people may not like this, but before sneering at the crudity of evolutionary "design," it may be wise to look carefully at the preposterous theological alternative tacitly espoused by Barash and ID theists. The flawlessly engineered world they prefer would be dead on delivery. Since it would already be perfect, it would also be finished; and if finished, it would have no future.

In other words, there could be no dramatic *transformation* going on in the kind of universe they idealize. Determined by a hypothetical intelligent designer to correspond impeccably in every detail to an eternally fixed master plan, such a world would be devoid of the contingency, indeterminacy, freedom, and futurity that give a truly dramatic character—and possibly a meaning—to evolution and the larger world process.

If you are the kind of theist or atheist who demands here and now a world with no design flaws, you are asking for an anemic idea of deity and a divine creation devoid of a deeper, dramatic coherence. If a fixed and frozen universe is what you want, then you may insist on perfect design as envisaged by ID and most contemporary evolutionary atheism. But if you prefer a truly surprising and richly creative universe, then you may be religiously open to evolution. Isn't it conceivable that Darwin's three-part recipe for evolution wells up from a hidden dramatic depth of nature wherein there resides an inaccessible wisdom that those obsessed with perfect design simply cannot fathom?

Christian belief, at any rate, does not depend for its credibility on the existence of a world without design flaws. Among notable Christian thinkers, Cardinal John Henry Newman (1801–90) expressed an exceptionally strong distaste for any theology that supports itself by leaning on the vapid criterion of design. Even before Darwin published the *Origin of Species*, Newman had written in 1852 that William Paley's design-oriented natural theology could "not tell us one word about Christianity proper," and that it "cannot be Christian, in any true sense, at all." Paley's brand of theology, Newman goes on, "tends, if it occupies the mind, to dispose it against Christianity." For Newman, in other words, it is not the task of theology to discover a divine designer lurking immediately beneath or behind the data of biology or physics.[7]

Furthermore, if you explore the Bible carefully, you will not find an elegant engineer there either. God's intimate relation to the world is before all else one of *liberation* and *promise* rather than the imposition of design. Consequently, any respectable theology after Darwin will not insist that the Creator is so petty as to function like an engineer tinkering mechanically with life. Theologians in the biblical tradition normatively understand divine creativity, providence, compassion, and wisdom as inseparable from the more basic motifs of liberation and promise, notions that do not correspond easily with that of engineering. Israel's idea of God is shaped above all else by its experience of the exodus from Egypt, and Christianity's God is inconceivable except in terms of the experience of being delivered from the most profound forms of enslavement, sin, and death. The God of Abraham and Jesus is a promising God, a God who seeks the transformation of all things, who dreams of renewal beyond the deep freeze of design, and who opens up the future even where it seems to mortals that there are dead ends everywhere.

It follows, therefore, that whenever the idea of God is separated from the conjugate themes of freedom and futurity, it is an idolatrous distortion, at least by biblical standards. This is why the engineer-God seems so remote from any genuinely biblical sense of the divine. At times, biblical metaphors, adapting to the popular imagination, may portray the Creator as an artisan, potter, builder, or planner. Such images serve to fortify believers' trust that their lives are not pointless and that goodness will prevail in the end. Yet only an extreme literalism can segregate these images from the dominant motifs of liberation and promise that frame the whole body of Hebrew and Christian reflection on God.

A properly biblical theology of nature will view divine wisdom, providence, and compassion less as a guarantee of the world's safety—as the idea of design encourages—than as an unbounded self-emptying graciousness that grants the world an open space and generous amount of time to become *more*, and in doing so gives it ample opportunity to participate in its own creative self-transformation. A God of freedom and promise invites, and does not compel, the creation to experiment with many possible ways of being, allowing it to make "mistakes" in the process. This is the God of evolution—one who honors and respects the indeterminacy and narrative openness of creation, and in this way ennobles it.

The God of evolution is a humble, self-donating liberality that avoids any unmediated manipulation of things. So, contrary to what Barash states, in the creation of life's diversity, it is not a matter of natural processes *rather than* God doing all the work, but of God creating through a drama of nature that is not "designed" to immediate perfection, but seeded with promise and potential for indeterminate outcomes, including the eventual emergence of human freedom. Theology's proper engagement with Darwinian science, therefore, need not be limited to a defense of suffocating notions of design. Theology after Darwin is much more interested in the drama that is still working itself out in nature.

But where is the drama going, if indeed it is going anywhere at all?

Chapter 6

Direction

There is grandeur in this view of life.
                    —*Charles Darwin,* The Origin of Species[1]

*What exhilarates us human creatures more than freedom, more than
the glory of achievement, is the joy of finding and surrendering to a
Beauty greater than man, the rapture of being possessed.*
                    —*Pierre Teilhard de Chardin*[2]

The teleology of the universe is its aim toward beauty.
                    —*Alfred North Whitehead*[3]

*D*oes the drama of evolution have any direction to it? Is the story of life
heading somewhere? Is there a goal toward which it is gradually wending
its way?

If we measure the movement of life in terms of a narrow human preoccupation with design, evolution seems blind and aimless. Because useful
adaptations arise opportunistically from a lottery of mostly nonadaptive
experiments, they are nearly always imperfect. Adaptive design appears to
be accidental, unforced, undirected. Consequently, most Darwinians, including Darwin himself, have assumed that *absence of directionality* is part of
the very definition of evolution. Scientists today usually agree. For instance,
the late Harvard paleontologist Stephen Jay Gould (1941–2002) repeatedly
insisted that evolution is like a randomly branching bush. If the tree of life
were replanted from seed, he surmised, it would not produce the same twigs
next time around, including our own species.[4]

Paleontologist Simon Conway Morris argues instead that evolution is
not so utterly gone wild as Gould supposed. Living organisms evolve along

convergent pathways that lead different lines of descent toward similar adaptive solutions. For example, saberlike predatory teeth, camera-like eyes, wings for flight, prehensile tails, sticky tongues, agricultural skills, a degree of intelligence, and many other analogous adaptive traits show up in a variety of species descended from genetically unrelated lineages. Geographically and temporally separated habitats often give rise independently to analogous adaptive solutions. Sooner or later, therefore, evolution would likely also have given rise to highly intelligent beings like us. Our existence may not be quite as unpredictable as Gould claimed.[5]

Conway Morris finds this "convergent" tendency of evolution to be theologically significant, but most evolutionary naturalists do not. Most of them agree with biologist S. E. Luria that "the essence of biology is evolution, and the essence of evolution is the absence of motive and purpose."[6] Much earlier than either Gould or Conway Morris, the famous evolutionist George Gaylord Simpson (1902–84) had expressed the sentiments of most Darwinians about the significance of human existence: in *The Meaning of Evolution* (1949), he declared that "man is the result of a purposeless and natural process that did not have him in mind. He was not planned."[7] Simpson acknowledged that we human beings are able to make plans and have purposes, but purpose was absent from the universe and evolution until we came along. Human beings may have "purpose on the brain," as Richard Dawkins puts it, but as a whole, nature is aimless.[8]

Darwin himself considered evolution to be blindly directionless, but he went along with the evolutionary philosopher Herbert Spencer in claiming that life can make a kind of "progress." After all, the fact that a species capable of refined moral sensitivity has finally emerged from an amoral animal ancestry is proof enough that evolution is not devoid of respectable outcomes. However, to Darwin and most evolutionists today, blind and aimless natural selection is sufficient to account for any such advances. No internal spiritual principle is pushing or pulling evolution toward a predetermined goal. It is only by way of chance and blind selection that impersonal evolution gradually settles on such remarkable inventions as human beings endowed with adaptive minds and morals. This naturalistic interpretation of evolution remains standard in the intellectual world today.

However, G. G. Simpson's colleague and friend, the Jesuit geologist Pierre Teilhard de Chardin (1881–1955), was not satisfied with the bald declaration that evolution is devoid of any overall purpose. Like Darwin, he allowed generously for the play of chance and large numbers in evolutionary innovation and adaptation, but he was also convinced that evolution moves in a measurable direction and that its directionality is suggestive of a subtle but effective divine principle of care quietly operative in the narrative marrow of the universe and life. The drama of life is a cumulatively transformative process in which something of utmost importance is taking place, even if analytical science cannot see it. Something of everlasting significance is working itself out in the universe and especially in the emergent stages of life, even though the coarse instruments of science are unable to register it.

Life, Teilhard points out, has clearly moved directionally in its evolution from less-complex to more-complex states of being. Why has there been any increase in organized physical complexity at all? It is not enough to reply that complexity is the only direction in which simplicity may move. For it is not unreasonable to imagine a universe or even a multiverse that remains stuck in a state of triviality forever. So why did life embark on its adventure of complexification when the universe may very well have been such as to allow it to remain perpetually in the state of a sheer dispersal of single cells (as it did for several billion years)?

Science can certainly give its own answers to these questions. Various specialists may reply, for example, that the principles of thermodynamics, biochemistry, and Darwinian selection can account for why life has become increasingly more complex over the past several billion years, and these answers would be correct. However, as Teilhard was inclined to ask, do the usual scientific answers rule out the pervasive presence and effectiveness of a noncoercive divine principle of directionality at work in the depths of life's drama? This is the theological question I would like to discuss with Darwin and his followers in the present chapter.

If natural selection can account for the movement of life from simple cells to brainy humans, does this mean that God has nothing to do with such an amazing set of emergent results? Dawkins would insist that God has nothing to do with it, but Darwin would not be quite so certain. I somehow doubt that Darwin would reject my use of "layered explanation" to make the point that scientific explanations are not necessarily opposed to theological accounts. If you recall, the fact that the chemistry of ink and paper can explain why words appear on this page does not exclude the fact that they also show up here because, at a deeper level of causation, the author wants to communicate his thoughts to you. Similarly, the fact that natural selection produces design, diversity, and what Darwin calls the "descent of man" does not exclude the possibility that the evolutionary drama carries a hidden meaning and that it is directional in a very profound sense because it bears invisibly within it the cooperative influence of a liberating and promising God. Darwin would rightly deny that science itself can detect any directionality in evolution, but, as far as I know, he was not so dogmatic as to claim that science is the only possible way to understand the dramatic depths of life.

Dawkins, however, keeps asking: Where is the evidence—and here he clearly means scientifically available evidence—of any divine principle of meaning and directionality in life? If a deity is involved in the unfolding of events in nature, why can't the chemist or evolutionary biologist see any sign of such activity? The answer, one that Dawkins will not accept, is that scientific method is simply not supposed to detect divine influence even if there is any. Just as a purely chemical analysis of this page cannot possibly detect the influence of the author's intention in the specific arrangement of words and sentences, so also evolutionary biology and biochemistry could never by themselves discover any possible meaning inscribed in the cosmic story or in life's unfolding. Meaning or purpose simply cannot show up at the level of scientific analysis. As far as Dawkins is concerned, science is powerful enough in its cognitional sweep to answer every conceivable question about the natural world. But this is a belief for which there can be no scientific evidence, and it is one that demands from science a kind of insight that it cannot in principle ever provide.

If God is involved in evolution, in any case, this involvement can be expressed only in the language of analogy, symbol, myth, and metaphor. The nature and depth of God's relationship to evolution, I suggest, is as inaccessible to the science of biology as the meaning on this page is to the equations of chemistry. The layers of causality operative in the production of this page, such as those of chemical reactions on the one hand and the author's intention on the other, are not mutually exclusive, but the author's intention will never show up in an analysis of the chemistry of ink and paper. Understanding chemistry is helpful, especially if the ink fails to bond with paper, but chemical expertise can tell you nothing about what the author is trying to say here.

To account, in any adequate way, for the existence of this page, you cannot leave out the fact that an author's intention lies behind it. But to grasp the author's meaning, you have to move beyond the level of chemical explanation to a deeper reading level, to where the discerning of meaning and intention comes into play. To do this, you must learn a completely different kind of skill from the kinds used by physical science. You must go through an initiation process, a transformation of consciousness, that opens up a whole new way of attending to and interpreting the kind of content the author is expressing.

My point is that every process or set of events can be read at different levels of comprehension, and each reading level leaves out content that others include. For example, reading this page at the level of chemistry leaves out any concern for the author's intentions in writing it, but this does not mean that no such intention is operative here. Analogously, can we be sure that there is no deep intentionality or purpose hidden in the dramatic depths of life and the universe just because the methods of science don't pick up any signals of it?

As I suggested in the preceding chapter, the dramatic aspect of life requires a kind of discernment different from that employed by chemistry and biology. If so, then knowing a lot about how natural selection works may be useful, but it will not tell you what life is really all about. Are you to assume that what Jesus or the Buddha had to say about life has now been rendered insignificant because of the arrival of biochemistry or evolutionary biology? That would be like saying, "Now that we have the chemical expertise to understand the way ink bonds with paper, there is no need to look for an author's intention as having anything important to do with this page's existence."

No analogy is adequate, however, so let me try another one, not that of chemical but one of grammatical analysis. If evolution has the shape of a drama, let us compare evolutionary science to the discovery and formulation of the rules of grammar that are necessary for the expression of the drama's possible meaning or direction. For Dawkins, to understand what life is really all about, all you need to look at closely are the neo-Darwinian rules that program populations of genes to be carried into the next generation. I suggest, however, that what Dawkins calls "genes" are like a lexicon, and the principles of gene selection are comparable to the grammatical rules that generate new versions of genetic word arrangements in the story of life.

The idea that evolution has to do with the migration of gene populations is unobjectionable, as Dawkins's own work allows us to see. However, Dawkins believes that the evolutionary grammar alone takes us all the way to the bottom of any thoroughgoing attempt to understand the life-process. I do not in any way wish to minimize the importance of gene-centered biology, or even of Dawkins's important contributions to it, but his claim strikes me as comparable to saying that what this page is *really* all about is not its author's meaning but the grammatical rules that shape my words and sentences.

It is accurate to say, surely, that natural selection "explains" the design, descent, and diversity of life. In a similar way it is accurate to say that the rules of grammar "explain" the arrangement of words and the structure of sentences on this page. But explaining this page in depth requires that you look at other explanatory levels also. Adherence to grammatical rules is obviously essential for my communication of meaning to you, the reader, but the specific content or meaning inscribed on this page is not determined by these rules. Meaning must be expressed in conformity with the rules of grammar, but knowledge of grammar alone is not enough to comprehend the meaning. My writing on this page has to "adapt" to the rules of syntax and sentence structure, but neither the meaning of my message nor my style of expressing it is straitjacketed by these "environmental" regulations.

Grammatical constraints, inflexible though they seem to be, do not prohibit the free expression of a wide range of ideas and meanings. Indeed, inflexible rules at the (lower) level of grammar help make the expression of an indeterminate range of meanings possible at the (higher) level of intellectual content. If I failed to obey the hard rules of grammar, you could make no sense of what I'm saying. You may not be able to do so anyway, but I don't think it's because I'm being ungrammatical. I'm simply suggesting that the unfolding of life also has to adhere to the "grammatical" rules that evolutionary biology has been successfully laying out for a century and a half. But if, as I argued in the previous chapter, life is a transformative drama, knowledge of the rules operative in gene transmission will tell you absolutely nothing about the drama's possible meaning.

Learning the rules of grammar is useful, but you do not need to be a grammarian to read and understand what I'm saying here. For centuries, indeed, readers with no formal knowledge of grammar have been able to grasp the meaning of literature profoundly and accurately. It may be a good thing that, after Noam Chomsky, we realize that the syntactical rules innate in human brains generate the structure of human language, but learning about these rules is not essential to an in-depth understanding of, say, Shakespeare's *Hamlet*. No matter how profound *Hamlet* is, or how creative Shakespeare may be, the drama must not violate the inflexible rules of grammar. But the meaning transcends the grammatical rules, and knowing what these rules are will never be enough to let you grasp the profundity of the drama itself.

Evolutionary biology and theology, analogously, may be looked upon as distinct levels of reading the drama of life. They are not rivals competing for your allegiance. Knowing that life is shaped by natural selection is one level, comparable to that of discovering the rules of grammar. Trying to understand what the story of life is about is another. And just as the meaning expressed on this page does not show up in grammatical analysis, so also any theologically interesting meaning the life-story might have cannot manifest itself in the formal concepts of Darwinian biology. Discerning any deeper meaning in the struggle, striving, success, and failures in life requires another kind of interpretative skill than that of expertise in scientific method.

In the drama of life, as I have pointed out several times before, we are dealing with the "the logic of achievement," as Polanyi calls it, where success and failure come into the picture. At this level of reading the life-story, learning how natural selection works is not essential to a poet's or prophet's grasp of the dramatic *depths* of life. Yes, it is good to know that natural selection has caused life to become more complex over time, just as it is good to know that innate grammatical rules generate the sentences on this page. However, understanding these grammatical rules will not be of much help as you try to understand and evaluate the content of this book. Likewise, understanding how natural selection generates adaptive design, diversity, and descent will not help you dig very deeply into the possible meaning of the drama of life. Nor will it help you answer the question of whether the universe is moving in a purposeful direction.

Life's Adventure

So what is the life-drama really all about? Can we speak of it as having a direction? Only, I believe, in the sense that a drama moves toward some kind of ending that may bring eventual coherence to its moments and episodes. But since the drama of life is still in process, and since Christians believe that it plays itself out ultimately within the mysterious theater of God's own timing, who are we to say right now what possible sense it all makes? Are we in a favorable position to say what life and its evolution are really all about?

Perhaps we are not completely in the dark here; so let me propose a tentative Christian theological reading, just as a modest point of departure. Without in any way contradicting biology, a theology of evolution may take note, first, of the fact that the general drift of life has been in the direction of increasing complexity, consciousness, and freedom. And the movement of evolution toward such outcomes has occurred without any suspension of the set of "grammatical constraints" that go by the name of "natural selection." Second, theology may attest that in its overall advance, what this drama is about is the liberation of nature from an endless imprisonment in lifeless and mindless determinism. Third, since the God of boundless love revealed in Jesus influences nature by way of attraction rather than force, a Christian theology of evolution may assume that God enlivens and gives meaning to the world not by pushing it forward from the past, but by calling it into the freshness of an always new future. And fourth, the "purpose" of the evolutionary drama consists, at the very minimum, of the intensification of creation's beauty, a beauty that, to Christian faith, is everlastingly sustained and patterned anew within the life of God.

Moreover, theology is comfortable with the idea that something significantly transformative is *still* going on in evolution. Any sense that theology at the present moment may have of life's possible future course and ultimate destiny, however, can only be extremely vague and general. Indeed, to be too specific would only diminish life's mystery and breadth. Not everything in the drama of evolution can be expected to move forward in military lockstep or in accordance with our own extremely limited understanding of the world at present. There will be digressions, waste, and blind alleys as the drama unfolds. Adaptations, including "convergent" adaptive solutions, will seldom if ever be totally suited to their environments, and organisms will always have design flaws. Any direction that evolution may have will not follow the narrow trajectory of a straight arrow launched fourteen billion years ago. There will be a trial-and-error aspect to it all, and not all experiments will work. Life will always be a struggle, allowing for either success or failure. There will also be abundant suffering and death (see chap. 8).

Such facts as these are offensive to the puritanical perfectionism of design-obsessed atheists and ID theists alike. Both parties think that a divine creator, if there is one, should at least live up to the exacting standards of human engineering efficiency. However, a theology of evolution judges the universe's and life's trajectories by the more elastic criteria of dramatic transformation rather than the stiffer and lifeless standards of design. Theology is impressed by a creation that, during its dramatic flowering, can maximize the values of creativity, relationship, freedom, courage, hope, love, and perhaps above all, the capacity of beings to make and keep promises. A perfectly designed and rigidly directed cosmos would be inconsistent with the emergence and thriving of such adventurous outcomes.

Order and design are values too, but if nature were perfectly designed, it could never give rise to the drama of life. Why not? Because, as the evolutionary philosopher Henri Bergson (1859–1941) observes, a perfectly prefabricated design for the world would close it off from ever having any *real* future.[9] If design and direction were to rule from the start, there would be no room for novelty and dramatic suspense. The universe would still be a fixed state, not a transformative story. Nor could it ever give rise to life. After all, life feeds on the indeterminate future even as it adheres to changeless "grammatical constraints" at each phase. Life strives to actualize *new* possibilities, and these can arise only out of the realm of the "not yet." Evolution, I would add, points to the indefiniteness of the "up ahead," the dwelling place of the promising God, who is the world's ultimate future and its lure toward more encompassing and always surprising beauty.

Theology, therefore, is happy to learn from Darwin that design does not dominate, for design without room for deviation is a prescription for morbidity. In a perfectly engineered universe, whatever comes next would already have been set in stone by what came before. There would be no real transformation but only a reshuffling of parts. A tightly drawn map of where evolution *must* lead would be inconsistent with the freshness and spontaneity of real life. For this reason theology may rejoice in the existence of a universe that allows for the ways, waste, and waywardness of evolution. Without considerable latitude for experimentation, all vitality would be squeezed out of this world. So would human freedom and creativity.

Making sense of evolution, therefore, requires that theology tentatively, and in a spirit of exploration rather than dogmatic certitude, inquire where the drama of life might be going rather than cataloging its success or failure in producing perfect instances of adaptive design. The question is not whether the world's creator can perform astounding design tricks, but whether anything of lasting significance might be working itself out dramatically in the universe as it undergoes its various phases of emergence and evolution.

Nature's dramatic depth, not its ephemeral organic arrangements, is the proper focus of a theology of evolution. However, evolutionary atheists, who have a habit of presenting themselves as experts on what an acceptable theology should look like, remain firm in their quest for perfect design as the only acceptable signal of cosmic purpose or God's existence. Along with their creationist and ID opponents, they are prepared to accept only a theology in which an omnipotent magician flashes improbable arrangements of organic molecules and complex systems. They will be satisfied only with a deity who leaves spectacular, scientifically accessible "evidence" of engineering competence. If God exists, they insist, design would be impeccable and life's direction inerrant. However, they never consider what this perfectionist dream would imply if it were ever actualized. It scarcely occurs to them that their idealized divine conjurer would produce only artifacts suitable for a display, not a drama featuring the struggle of life and the transformation of the entire universe into more interesting, if dangerous, modes of existence.

A Christian theology of evolution, for its part, looks for an alternative to the rigor mortis of perfect design, and this is why Darwin's depiction of life is not so distressing after all. Theologically understood, biological evolution is part of a great cosmic journey into the incomprehensible mystery of God. The various fields of research that contribute to evolutionary science (for example, geology, paleontology, comparative anatomy, embryology, biogeography, and genetics) all have their own special approach to the story of life on earth, but so also does theology. Perhaps life, at a dramatic level inaccessible to the mathematical abstractions of physical science, is an adventure stirred up by a God of persuasive love, as philosopher Alfred North Whitehead has proposed. Under the influence of a divine tenderness too refined to be captured by mathematical analysis, life aims toward the intensifying of feeling, enjoyment, consciousness, freedom, responsiveness—and increasingly intense forms of beauty.

Whitehead did not expect scientists to see life in this dramatic way, since every science is limited by its own methodological constraints. Just as we don't expect the grammarian to be an expert on *Hamlet*, we don't expect any particular field of science to produce a deep sense of the meaning of life and its evolution. From a Christian theological point of view, however, life and evolution are the universe's response to the presence and promise of divine persuasive love. A drama of transformation is going on in creation and—because of the divine incarnation—this drama is also taking place within the life of God. Life is the story of a divinely inspired struggle by creation to realize something of great and everlasting consequence: the transformation of the universe, and human existence along with it, into the dwelling place of the incarnate God. Christian teaching entails nothing less than the world's divinization. Moreover, the resurrection of Christ is the promise not only of our own survival after death, but even more fundamentally, of the redemptive transfiguration of the whole material universe by the author of life.

If life has such a transformative meaning, it would grasp us much more than we could ever grasp it. This is why it is so difficult ever to say clearly and exactly, or here and now, what that meaning might be. Stories are the appropriate medium for expressing profound meaning, but we must allow a story to carry us away, as it were, in order to be touched by its import. Science does not look for narrative meaning, so we need not expect from the evolutionary biologist any profound commentary on what the drama of life is really all about. The evolutionary biologist can specify the rules life has to follow. But just as a grammarian would focus only on the rules of writing operative on this page, and not on its meaning, a neo-Darwinian biologist would try to understand the genetic principles and selection pressures at work in life across many generations. The evolutionary scientist as such is not obliged to look for any deeper significance to evolution. However, Richard Dawkins, whose work on the "selfish gene" may be of some help at the level of understanding evolution's grammatical rules, does not stop here. He in effect declares that beneath the grammar of life, there is no meaning at all. For him, life is not a drama but an "indifferent" succession of design flaws and imperfect adaptations. Life for this grammarian is not even significant enough to rise to the level of tragedy.

However, neither science nor theology can discount the fact that the cosmos has felt its way dramatically toward a net increase in complexity, vitality, sentience, consciousness, freedom, and moral sensitivity. By any standard of measurement, it is hard to deny that our universe has come a long way from the relative simplicity of primordial cosmic plasma to the nearly incalculable complexity of the human brain and cultural innovation. It would be highly arbitrary not to notice, or to disregard as insignificant, this transformative directionality. The universe is neither pure contingency nor pure necessity. It is a blend of openness, reliability, and temporal depth that endow it with a narrative quality completely unnoticed by the design-obsessed and grammar-fixated. I hasten to add here that the possible existence of innumerable universes (a multiverse) would only enlarge, not eliminate, the dramatic character of creation and evolution. Questions about the overall meaning of a multiverse would be as relevant and alive as they are for our own universe and its unfolding in time.

Like it or not, in our big bang universe at least, the evidence shows that since life's beginning almost four billion years ago, evolution has been feeling its way toward more intensely conscious kinds of being. Is this purely by accident or purely by necessity? Or is it the product of the blend of contingency, law, and time that makes nature an adventurous narrative and not a mere succession of states? The biologist will be satisfied—and rightly so, scientifically speaking—to explain the emergence of mind simply as the product of natural selection. But a layered approach to explanation can add that, at another reading level, the dramatic arrival of mind and freedom in life's evolution is due to the noncoercive lure of an infinitely good and wise divine presence completely hidden to Darwinian grammarians. Without any conflict with physical, chemical, or biological readings of life, theology may reasonably propose that a deeper transformative principle has been quietly inviting the cosmic process toward such momentous outcomes all along, and that it has been doing so without intruding into or interrupting natural processes that, at the level of a purely scientific understanding, seem to be altogether devoid of any deep significance.

"Why hasn't science found *evidence* of divine influence?" will be the persistent objection of the evolutionary naturalist. However, just as knowledge of grammar is not enough to catch the dramatic meaning of *Hamlet*, scientific method is too crude an instrument to detect the subtlety of any divine inspiration that might be at work in the dramatic depths of evolution. Indeed, why would we want science to be able to detect such a dimension of depth anyway? We don't expect grammarians to speak authoritatively about the content of a tragic or comic drama. So we should not expect either Darwin or Dawkins to tell us what evolution is *ultimately* all about either, even though Dawkins, unlike Darwin, insists on telling us anyway.

What is needed is a more refined kind of "seeing," as Teilhard emphasizes, one that looks to the "insideness" of things. Only a nonanalytical way of experiencing, once that goes beyond mere measurement and quantitative analysis, could ever come in touch with life's dramatic depth. Beneath the external, mechanical causality that science deals with, there is a *narrative cosmological principle* operative in the universe as such. It shapes events not in the manner of an architect or engineer, but of a dramatist that allows the characters to take on lives of their own. Operating in the manner of unrelenting love, this dramatic principle beckons the creation to rise toward the begetting of innumerable diverse states of being, including consciousness and responsibility. Since scientific method looks only to the "outside" of things, the deeply interior drama in the domain of life goes unnoticed by the evolutionary grammarian. It is the proper role of a theological reading, however, to point readers of nature to the adventurous narrative of love and liberation at work beneath the surface available to science.

Waiting

Stories, not static structures, are the main vehicles of meaning, and stories require time—sometimes an enormous amount of it—to disclose their content. Evolution is a story, not a state, and since the story is still unfolding we cannot expect to know yet, with any close-up clarity, exactly what it is all about. We have to wait patiently and hopefully, along with all of life. Life loses its narrative deportment, and any profound meaning, whenever we try to repackage it into patterns of immediately decipherable design. If the mystery of life were ever fully translated into the categories of engineering and architecture, it would no longer have a meaning. It might have an interesting shape but not a profound significance. Creationists, intelligent design advocates, and materialist evolutionists all miss this point. They demand immediate contemporary comprehension when what is needed is a more realistic posture of waiting for the drama of life to unfold its meaning. The fatal flaw of both antievolutionist religious ideology and materialist evolutionism is their crass impatience, their acquisitiveness about reaching absolute clarity here and now.

Meanwhile, the narrative depth of life eludes all demands for immediate transparency. The quest for unambiguous evidence of perfect design in living beings scarcely conceals a longing that all of reality should come to a dead stop so that it can be captured and mastered by objectifying analysis. A greedy insistence that the whole of nature and life must present itself to our voracious demand for instantaneous intelligibility is a symptom of all world-shrinking ideology, whether religiously fundamentalist or scientifically materialist. In this respect Daniel Dennett, Richard Dawkins, David Barash,

Jerry Coyne, and other evolutionary materialists I have mentioned are not as distant from their ID enemies as they may think. In the tedious debate about God and design, both sides want to reduce the question of life's having any overall meaning, and even that of whether the universe has a purpose, to the simplistic puzzle over whether adaptive design in living beings reveals the face of God right now—without any ambiguity. Adopting the biblical caution that no one can see the face of God and live (Exod. 33:20), an evolutionary theology, on the other hand, does not expect the world to work this way.

If life is a drama, it transpires at a level of reality much deeper than anything that could be captured in the abstract mathematical constructs of science or in graphic contemporary models of perfectly engineered design. If life, at bottom, is a transformative narrative, then the human mind cannot readily connect with it apart from adopting the posture required to appreciate any dramatic unfolding of events. Such a posture above all includes a willingness to wait. It is those who wait for the Lord who "will never be put to shame" (cf. Ps. 25:3 NASB). And if the drama is still unfolding, it is out of place for anyone to demand that its meaning, or lack thereof, display itself forthwith. The question of whether evolution makes theological sense cannot be reduced to that of whether life conforms to our contemporary standards of decent design. Any coherence that a drama might have simply cannot manifest itself until it is fully told, and this requires time. If life is a drama, its final meaning may be only just dawning, and hence it would lie largely unavailable to both scientific and theological comprehension at the present moment.

If the drama of life has a meaning, it is only in the future, not the present or the past, that it would let itself be known since only then could things come together in a coherent way. If human inquiry looks exclusively to the cosmic past for complete understanding, as scientific analysis typically does, nature and life fall apart into the dust of isolated cells, molecules, and atoms. Analysis alone leaves the world incoherent, scattered about in unconnected bits. Scientific reduction can lead to a clear sense of the world's elemental units, but not to any inkling of its possible coherence. This is why a theology of evolution must insist that if the story of life in the universe possesses an overall purpose, it would not become evident to any present-time or past-oriented scientific reading. To apprehend evolution's meaning, you would need to turn around and face toward the future. You would have to wait.

To understand what I mean, try out the following exercise. Picture yourself standing on earth about 3.8 billion years ago. This is about the time when the earliest living cells were appearing. As you journey even further back in time from this point in cosmic history, making your way slowly toward the horizon of the early universe, you will see living cells disintegrating into molecules, molecules into atoms, and atoms into subatomic elements. You will eventually arrive at a state of subatomic dispersal that materialized not long after the Big Bang. Then, after having made your way all the way back to this point, turn around and start moving forward in time toward the present. As you travel in this direction you will need to wait patiently until you see anything remarkable occurring. Eventually, however, you will see atoms forming and then very gradually being integrated into molecules, molecules into cells, cells very slowly fusing with one another into complex organisms, organisms developing backbones and complex nervous systems, brains appearing, and conscious beings eventually populating a planet.

You will notice, in other words, that coherence begins to show up only when you look *from* the fragmented cosmic past *toward* the more complex and unified states of being that emerge in the future. Now start looking from this present moment in natural history (the twenty-first century in terrestrial time) toward the cosmic future yet to occur. Again you will have to wait. You can't see anything clearly yet, but you have by now learned from your journey that the scattered elements dominant in the remote past acquired deeper meaning (coherence) only as you moved toward what came later. If you were willing to keep moving patiently into the future, you would discover what an atom, molecule, or cell could *really* become when it eventually merged into association and integration with other elements, and then later became taken up into even more comprehensive systems. From the very beginning of the big bang universe, surely, the physical conditions and constants had to have the mathematical values that would allow for eventual complex coherence. The universe is seeded with the promise of emergent coherence from the outset. But a promise requires patience, hope, and trust as we look toward its final fulfillment.

What can you learn from this exercise? That if the cosmic process and evolution have a meaning—that is, if they have any overall coherence—you cannot expect to find it here and now by looking only at design, or by breaking complex instances of design down into their elementary components or into past states of atomic, molecular, and cellular units, no matter how interesting such reduction may be. To be in a position to look for evolution's overall coherence, and hence its possible meaning, you need to condition your mind to look from the past toward what is still emerging up ahead, in the future. However, this way of seeing requires that you go beyond science and assume a stance of anticipation, though without in any way contradicting scientific analysis. It may require that you put on the virtue of hope.

Purpose

While you are waiting for the future, can you at least catch a glimpse of what might be dawning by looking at what has already happened? In evolution's errant ramblings and serendipitous escapades, is an overall narrative coherence already beginning to take shape? Are there at least some hints that might arouse a reasonable hope that there may be a final meaning to the drama? In life's gradual emergence, is there some vague "evidence," even here and now, of its having at least a loosely directional drift?

To have a meaning, the drama of life must all along have been more than just aimless meandering. Something of importance (or value) must already have shown itself as the drama develops, though perhaps fleetingly and ambiguously. Looking for such importance in the evolution of life is the same as looking for purpose. By "purpose," I mean that something of undeniable value or significance is coming into being. So, to interpret a process as purposeful, we would have to witness that in its overall unfolding something of great significance is already working itself out. In the case of evolution, what could that be?

The dimension of drama excavated by Darwin's work provides at least a small part of an answer. Evolution's meaning, we may surmise at least in a vague and general way, somehow consists of its adventurous aim to intensify *beauty* or what Darwin called "grandeur" in the universe. "The teleology [purpose] of the universe," as Whitehead puts it, "is its aim toward beauty."[10] From a Christian perspective, much more is no doubt going on in evolution than this, but at the very least the drama of life, along with the cosmic process as a whole, has had the net effect of leaning toward the intensification of beauty, and this is enough to give it at least a baseline directionality.

During the last century the narrative aspect of nature that had already begun to emerge in the fields of geology and biology was eventually extended so as to embrace the entire universe. Relativity theory, big bang cosmology, and astronomy have now clearly demonstrated that the universe is still a work in progress. With Whitehead, I want to suggest that what is going on in the cosmic story and more recently in life's evolution is an ongoing aim toward the maximizing of beauty. The cosmos, at the very least, has been undergoing an aesthetic transformation. The process is not always straightforward, and long periods pass in which nothing terribly dramatic seems to happen. But over the long haul, banality has been supplanted by beauty, mere elements by elaborate elegance. In its adventurous struggle toward what Darwin rightly calls grandeur, nature turns out to be something profoundly purposeful.

Purpose means the actualizing of something good, important, or valuable, and beauty may be the most sublime of all values. Beauty, in its Whiteheadian definition, means the harmony of contrast or, better, the ordering of novelty. Since "purpose" can be defined as the actualizing of value, nature's purpose consists, minimally, of its ageless urge to intensify forms of ordered novelty. If so, then the meaning of our own lives within the larger drama of the universe and evolution may have something to do with our contributing in our own small but unique ways to the intensification of the world's beauty. The great wisdom traditions may add their own distinct shades of meaning to this mysteriously transformative aesthetic drama that goes by the name "cosmos," of which the life-story comprises the most interesting set of episodes. However, the various religious traditions may discover beneath all doctrinal differences the silent but persistent cosmic quest for an ultimate beauty—in other words, for "Perfection."

The actualizing of beauty during the Darwinian chapters in the cosmic story gradually takes on the shape of heightening consciousness, self-awareness, freedom, moral sensitivity, aesthetic enjoyment, and the instinct to worship. A process that can bring about beings endowed with these traits is not trivial. Indeed, it is literally mind blowing. So there is no rational basis for arbitrarily asserting that evolution is aimless when in fact it has already accomplished something so wonderful.

Beauty, Whitehead says, arises from the harmonizing of contrasts and the ordering of novelty. Things that manifest beauty do so because they hold these polar elements in creative tension. Unfortunately, evolutionary materialists associate purpose almost exclusively with order or design, not with the fact of emergent novelty. They look for purpose not in the aesthetic drama of beauty's precarious emergence, but in their idealization of a fixed and perfect design, which never shows up in evolution. Disappointed by the deficiencies in the many instances of adaptive design, they feel compelled to tell the rest of us that nature must be purposeless and godless. They virtually ignore the fact that novelty is continually pouring into the world, stirring it toward an adventurous, dramatic, transformative, but still unfinished experimentation with fresh forms of beauty, not excluding the majesty of their own minds. They fail to notice that all evolutionary experiments with imperfect "design" are part of the larger, aesthetically richer, ongoing, and more interesting drama of life.

Making sense of evolution, therefore, requires that we look at the long drama of emergent beauty more vigilantly than at the more trivial instances of present design. The interesting theological question is not why there exist so many imperfect examples of intricate adaptive design, but why the universe is a dramatic adventure of aesthetic transformation at all. Theologically understood, the ultimate source of the novelty, which gives an aesthetic dimension to the drama of life and to the entire universe, is what biblical writings refer to as "God." In the Bible, God is not just the ground of order but also the source of novelty and surprise. Second Isaiah (Isa. 42:9) as well as Revelation (21:5), for example, explicitly present us with a God who makes all things new. For the apostle Paul (Gal. 6:15), what matters is that what God brings about in Christ is *new* creation. Classical theology, however, has unfortunately associated God primarily with cosmic order and failed to acknowledge adequately the connection between God and novelty. Evolutionary biology and cosmology, on the other hand, now require that if we think about God at all, it must be as the ultimate source of dramatic novelty, not just the upholder of fixed order. God, in other words, is the lure that awakens the universe to become a transformative adventure, liberating it from the monotony and inertia of fixed and frozen design.

The world's aim toward beauty, however, is constantly frustrated not only by an entropic tendency to collapse into chaos but also by a tendency at times to remain stuck in monotony when further aesthetic transformation is still possible. As Whitehead observes, the cosmic aim is toward more intense beauty, toward richer syntheses of order and novelty. So acquiescence in pure order without novelty runs contrary to a robust understanding of cosmic purpose. This is another reason why an evolutionary theology insists that thinking of God only in terms of fixed design is shallow and shortsighted.

A theology of evolution, moreover, is not interested in defending the idea of a God who is thought of only as the source of design since this would only make us wonder why the "designer" does not immediately eliminate the disorder of suffering in the drama of life. Nor is an evolutionary theology interested in thinking of God exclusively as the source of novelty, since novelty without order is mere chaos. After Darwin and Einstein, a good way to think about God is as the ultimate source of ordered novelty, as a disturbing lure that seeks to intensify the world's beauty. "God's purpose in the creative advance," Whitehead says, "is the evocation of intensities."[11] Such a God is not interested in perpetuating the status quo but in making the universe become more than what it is now. It becomes more, however, especially by intensifying its beauty and the aesthetic capacity of beings to enjoy this beauty.[12]

However, it seems that such an intensification of aesthetic capacity in the drama of life cannot take place without a corresponding increase in the capacity for suffering and the possibility of tragedy. Can a theology of evolution make sense of life's suffering? The answer, once again, is "not yet." If there were ever a question resistant to receiving a presently satisfying response, it is that of why the drama of life involves so much agony and loss. To make ourselves receptive to any answer at all, however, we must be prepared to wait. Such is the requirement of faith.

Meanwhile, Job's questions and complaints to his creator about the unfairness of life are as pressing as ever, and no closer, it would seem, to rationally soothing resolution. A contemporary Christian theology of evolution, however, may at least venture to say a bit more during our time of waiting. If, as our creeds profess, the compassionate picture of Jesus as the healing and promising redeemer is the revelatory key to understanding what God is like, then we are permitted, first, to assume that God does not directly cause suffering or want it to occur; and second, we are encouraged to hope that all suffering will be redeemed, including the suffering of nonhuman sentient life. What a good God wills directly cannot be suffering or death but the well-being of all creatures and the fulfillment of the whole universe. An infinite, wasteful, overflowing creative love wills not just being, but also *more* being, *more* beauty, *more* intensity of enjoyment. In the light of evolution and contemporary cosmology, God may be pictured as sponsoring the *maximizing* of beauty and aesthetic enjoyment in the created world.

Nevertheless, in the aesthetic adventure of appropriating novelty, each present instance of order runs the risk of disintegration. In the transition from triviality toward more intensity of beauty and capacity for enjoyment, there is always the risk of the evil of disorder, including excessive suffering. The cosmic adventure and the drama of life do not occur without such a risk. The creative advance that occurs in the cosmic process and especially in life's evolution, as Whitehead acknowledges, takes place along the borders of chaos.[13]

So it must be admitted that in maximizing the aesthetic intensity of the cosmos, God opens up the universe to a transformative drama that is not immune to tragic outcomes and episodes. If you do not like such a universe—an entirely understandable first reaction—it may be illuminating to think out thoroughly what your own alternative would entail. Your proposal might be to have God create a finished and fully perfected universe from day one of creation. But such a perfectly designed universe would have no room for life, freedom, and new being. An initially fixed and finished universe would have no future. It would also be insentient and mindless. This is the kind of universe you will end up with if you are obsessed with design and indifferent to drama.

If God had not opened up the universe to novelty and drama from the start, there would have been no suffering. But there would have been no increase in value (beauty), life, sentience, and consciousness either. In a perfectly designed universe, there would arise no need to wrestle with the "theodicy problem": the question of how to make sense of evil and suffering in a world said to have been created by a good and all-powerful God. A world devoid of evil and suffering may be a theoretically conceivable alternative to the one we have, but it would have been aesthetically trivial in comparison with the dramatically intense universe that is still coming into being and whose meaning remains obscure until the story is fully told.

Unwilling to settle for the triviality of the status quo, the God of Christian faith is concerned with the transformation of the world into an intensity of beauty whose eventual depth and scale are far beyond our reckoning. Immersed as we are in the drama of a still-unfolding creation here and now, we can only wait in hope for redemption (though not in a state of passivity, for there is work to be done). But it is only by taking on the virtue of hope that we can participate fully as humans in the ongoing drama of life. To despair would be equivalent to giving up on life and opting out of the adventure. In the evolutionary unfolding of life, in the whole universe's transformation into the extended body of Christ, and in its aim toward the perfection of beauty, suffering does occur. But so also, we may hope, does redemption. In the discussion of death in chapter 8, I will have more to say about how the prospect of redemption is still a reasonable hope as we dig deeper into the drama.

Chapter 7

Depth

The world is deep,
And deeper than the grasp of day.
Deep is its pain—,
Joy—deeper still than misery:
Pain says: Refrain!
Yet all joy wants eternity—
Wants deep, wants deep eternity.

—Friedrich Nietzsche[1]

There lives the dearest freshness deep down things.
—Gerard Manley Hopkins[2]

I have been saying that the drama of life lies at a deeper level than that of design, but this way of putting things assumes that there is a dimension of depth to evolution that usually goes unnoticed. It is part of Darwin's enormous contribution to theology that he has opened up an abyss into whose depth the design-obsessed, both Christian and atheist alike, have been reluctant to look. It is now time to follow Darwin's lead and look further down into this abyss.

Both science and religion assume that things are not what they appear to be.[3] This can only be because they must both at least tacitly sense that beneath the surface of our ordinary or commonsensical impressions of the world, there is something deeper. Because of his concern for putting us in touch with this dimension of depth, I shall invite Paul Tillich (1886–1965), an influential twentieth-century Christian theologian, to initiate this chapter's conversation with Charles Darwin.

Tillich—I shall let him speak in the present tense—is keenly aware that many scientists and scientifically educated philosophers, including evolutionists, now believe that human knowledge has outgrown the idea of God. He also thinks they may have a good reason for this impression. Before science came along, God was usually taken to be the direct cause of events in nature. If rains were gentle, sunshine plentiful, and peace prevalent, this was evidence of direct divine influence. And if earthquakes, captivities, and floods happened, these too were a sign of God's immediate action. In either case, God seemed to be an actor within the drama of history and nature. But belief in such a diminished deity, Tillich insists, can no longer survive, nor does it deserve to survive, especially in the age of science.

Science, especially after Darwin, has made it increasingly implausible to think of God as an actor or intervener in nature. In this respect, Tillich is happy to agree with Christianity's cultured critics. The fact that believers persist in linking God directly to special events in nature is one of the main reasons so many scientists find Christian faith incompatible with evolution. In a prescientific age, the sense of God understandably came to expression in oral traditions and scriptures that located divine action alongside natural causes; but in a scientific age, such reports cannot be taken literally. And as long as preachers, teachers, and theologians keep attributing natural phenomena—such as the emergence of complex adaptive design—to direct divine action, scientifically enlightened people, not unlike Darwin himself, will find it hard to embrace Christianity. For them, there is no need to speak of divine interventions or "special creation" in nature since natural explanations are sufficient at the level of simple cause-and-effect occurrences.

It is not only scientifically but also theologically objectionable, Tillich would add, to make God play such a reduced role. Situating divine action anywhere within a chain of natural causes means denying God's transcendence. Doing so is both scientifically self-defeating and religiously idolatrous. Thinking of God as a kind of cause that can eventually be replaced by scientific explanations is one of the main reasons for the rise of modern atheism. No wonder so many sincere people want nothing to do with theology.

Darwin himself was justified, Tillich would allow, in spurning the impoverished theology of his day. The God of "special creation" is so small as to be hardly worth defending in the first place. So if theology is to survive in the age of science, Tillich argues, it must find a more appropriate place to situate its references to God. Tillich's important contribution is to have us think of God not as an actor within nature, but as nature's "depth," "abyss," and "ground." With these earthy metaphors, he tries to show how, as science advances, speaking about God becomes more important rather than less important. This is because the very prospect of science having any future at all depends upon nature's having a dimension of depth yet to be explored. It is partly in terms of this depth that theology, especially in its conversations with Darwin, may speak of God and the drama of life.

In his famous sermon "The Depth of Existence," Tillich reflects on the fact that beneath the surface of our experience of other people, ourselves, and nature, there resides a region of fathomless profundity that we do not usually notice until an "earthquake" occurs. For example, we may think we know another person well, but this person may do something to shock, surprise, or disappoint us, and then we realize that we had only a shallow understanding of who that individual really is. So we must begin to relate to the other person at a deeper level than before.

Similarly, we generally have a relatively shallow understanding of ourselves. But inevitably crises occur in our personal lives that demand a deepening of our understanding of who we are. Our first reaction to a major disappointment—such as the death of a parent, or the loss of friends or our health—is often that of denial. But eventually we may discover a dimension of depth in our personal existence that gives us the courage to accept ourselves and go on with our lives in spite of loss, guilt, doubts, and the fact of our mortality. This courage is possible only if we come into encounter with a dimension of depth underlying our own existence, a depth that had previously lay hidden beneath the surface.

Nature also has a dimension of depth. Our relationship to nature is usually relatively shallow too, but occasionally a great genius comes along and invites us to look beneath nature's surface. The history of science provides many examples. Copernicus and Galileo dug beneath the commonsense understanding of the heavens on which Ptolemaic astronomy had been based. The Copernican revolution seemed to open up an abyss beneath the safe assumptions about nature that people had taken for granted for ages. The discoveries of Galileo dramatically disoriented ordinary people and popes alike. Churchmen and philosophers turned away from the evidence for terrestrial motion, retreating to the ancient idea of changeless heavens. Turning back toward what is familiar is a typical first response to any exposure to the dimension of depth.

The initial reaction to the new astronomy taking shape in the seventeenth century was often one of denial, but eventually the world of thought adjusted. More recently, science has discovered that the entire universe has a historical and narrative depth that nobody knew about several generations ago, and it is still hard for some people to accept the new cosmology. But by now the world of thought has at least begun to adjust to relativity, "deep time," and the new story of a fourteen-billion-year-old universe.

It is doubtful, however, that anything in the history of science has exposed the abyss beneath nature's surface more dramatically, nor caused so passionate a denial of nature's depth on the part of so many people, than has Darwin's theory of evolution. Indeed, many religious believers are still in denial. But so also are the evolutionary atheists, who have found it easier to focus on the relatively shallow theme of design than to look seriously into the deeper drama of life.

The Road to Depth

It is not easy for anyone to encounter the dimension of depth beneath the surface of our lives and thoughts. Tillich observes that the testimony of wise men and women throughout the ages tells about how difficult the road to depth can be. It is difficult because seekers of depth "have found that they were not what they believed themselves to be, even after a deeper level had appeared to them below the vanishing surface. That deeper level itself became surface, when a still deeper level was discovered, this happening again and again, as long as their very lives, as long as they kept on the road to their depth."[4] In reaction to the call to deepen our lives and thoughts, we usually allow ourselves to be distracted, preferring the safety of superficiality to the seriousness of what lies beneath the surface. However, a call from the depths is always there, attracting and inviting, even when we take flight from it. Both scientific and religious accounts of journeys into depth still grip us today because we can hear in them the challenge to ourselves to move toward a more profound way of being and understanding, an experience that can give meaning—and a surprising joy—to our own lives.

Can we give a name to the elusive but strangely compelling dimension of depth that lies beneath the surface of our lives and thoughts? Here is Tillich's answer:

> The name of this infinite and inexhaustible depth . . . is God. That depth is what the word God means. And if that word has not much meaning for you, translate it, and speak of the depths of your life. . . . Perhaps, in order to do so, you must forget everything traditional that you have learned about God, perhaps even that word itself. For if you know that God means depth you know much about Him. You cannot then call yourself an atheist or unbeliever. For you cannot think or say: Life has no depth! Life itself is shallow. Being itself is surface only. If you could say this in complete seriousness, you would be an atheist; but otherwise you are not. He who knows about depth knows about God.[5]

We cannot focus on this inexhaustible depth as though it were an object of scientific investigation. It is comparable to a horizon that keeps receding into the distance as we try to approach it. The dimension of depth always encompasses and illuminates everything we experience, but it never falls within our comprehending vision or intellectual control. Thus God—the inexhaustible dimension of depth beneath the surface of our lives and of nature—may seem absent or even nonexistent since we can have no "evidence" of depth in the scientific sense of an object available to empirical observation. The infinite depth is too expansive and too real to be gathered in by the finite human mind. It comprehends us more than we comprehend it. It is not reducible to a scientific hypothesis. Instead, it is what makes possible an endless revision of scientific hypotheses, and hence scientific progress.

The dimension of depth usually comes to our attention after experiencing "earthquakes" that open up an "abyss" beneath the surface of our lives and our customary intellectual assumptions. Darwin's new picture of life has proved to be just such an earthquake. Evolutionary science has laid bare a new level of depth in nature, life, and human existence. For many people, looking into the Darwinian depths seems at first like looking into a bottomless ravine. A typical reaction has been to shrink back, to turn their eyes away from the apparent emptiness that yawns beneath the kindly surface of nature. In the last century and a half, Darwin's picture of evolution has shaken the foundations of human understanding and opened up what seems, at least to many pious people, an endless void beneath what they had taken to be the firm foundation of benign providential design.

Similar experiences had already happened to religious believers as they learned about new scientfic discoveries even before Darwin. But it is clear that for many people today Darwin's science is especially abysmal; like every other abyss, it strangely continues to attract even while it repels. Is this perhaps because God awaits us there? Tillich, at least, would want us to ponder this possibility. God is both the abyss and the ground of being. The divine depth is ambiguous: beneath the abyss there is always more solid ground. So the initially shocking encounter with Darwin's view of life could lead to an adventurous exposure not only to the abyss but also to the ground of being, to God.

Obviously this is not the way most people approach the Darwinian picture of life. Not only creationists and ID Christians but also evolutionary materialists have yet to look deeply into the drama of life. Evolution is a stumbling block to the design-obsessed, whether they are devoutly religious or disciples of Dawkins. The manner in which natural selection works to bring about design, diversity, and descent does not conform to expectations of what nature should be like. So devout creationists and ID Christians on the one side, and militant atheistic evolutionists on the other—though seemingly far apart—both interpret Darwin's dissolving of design not as an invitation to move toward deeper (dramatic) ground but as an opening to the void of absurdity. For both sides, Darwin depicts a world that fails to match their idealization of architecturally perfect order. So evolution, if true, must mean the death of God.

Creationist and ID reaction to Darwin is a clear sign that evolution, at least for large numbers of people, provides the main entry these days to an abyss devoid of deity. Religious people turn away from this void by demonizing Darwin and denying the abundant evidence for evolution. Meanwhile, to many who accept evolution, "Darwinism" also goes best with atheism. Atheistic evolutionists boast that they have looked into the Darwinian depths and seen only proof of a wondrous but ultimately pointless universe. It is partly for this reason that Daniel Dennett considers Darwin's "dangerous idea" the most important in the history of thought. For him, it not only provides the deepest possible explanation of all kinds of living traits, including human behavior, but it functions as a "universal acid" that eats through every naive notion that life and the universe have any inherent meaning.[6] Dennett clearly thinks of himself as grown up enough to accept this blank cosmic void. His bedrock materialism allows him to claim that philosophy has finally bored all the way down to the foundational mindlessness underlying all of being.

However, Dennett's swaggering materialism is just another way of avoiding the Darwinian depths. He refuses to be captured by the challenging and bracing *drama* that still goes on beneath the rubble of shattered design. He wants his college sophomores to watch how he can survive and even thrive after swallowing the poison pill of naturalistic pessimism, and he promises to take his readers deeper than creationism and ID. But his quest for depth only lands in the spongy swamp of final meaninglessness. His journey into depth stops short of ever finding its way completely down through the abyss of chance, necessity, and deep time to the wondrous ground consisting of the cosmic narrativity that makes the drama of evolution possible in the first place.

The Two Faces of Depth

Darwin, whose own limited theological education had centered on design, knew his own discoveries would be deeply unsettling. He even wrote to a friend that going public with the notion of natural selection was like "confessing to a murder." Evolution, he must have realized, will expose people to a hitherto unnoticed abyss beneath the design that they assumed to have been securely fashioned by a divine creator in the beginning. Since Darwin uncovered an apparent abyss beneath the shallow surface of design, the natural instinct of religious believers has been to flinch and even close their eyes. It has led many to deny evolution altogether, for as design dissolves, the whole world seems to teeter on the brink of absurdity.

However, depth has two faces. It is not just abyss but also ground, terrifying at first, but ultimately liberating and redemptive. Looking earnestly into the depth of everything involves a kind of death, but it also promises resurrection. The breakdown of our narrow human ideals of design, as the book of Job had already made clear, is an abysmal experience. Yet it is the first step toward a wider and deeper sense of creation's beauty than we ever could have reached otherwise. Hence, challenges such as Darwin's to our constricted religious and ethical ideals of design should not come as an insurmountable difficulty, at least to a biblically grounded spiritual vision.

Christianity itself rose up from the ashes of a kind of design death. To his friends, Jesus' own execution seemed, at least at first, to prove only the powerlessness of God to carry out the divine plan. Nevertheless, the early Christian community eventually came to interpret Jesus' death by crucifixion as the decisive opening onto the final victory of life over death. The cross reveals to Christians, beneath all disillusionment with what we had taken to be a benign providential plan, the unsurpassable beauty of a self-sacrificing God, who draws near to the creation and embraces the struggles, failures, and achievements of the whole drama of life. Christians are invited to view all experiences of design death, including that introduced by Darwin, as entry into the abyss of the cross that God also bears, the cross through which one can be brought to the deep experience of resurrection. In the context of Christian faith, the drama of evolution merges inseparably with the (abysmal) death and (grounding) resurrection of Jesus and, in him, with the eternal drama that is the Trinitarian life of God.

However, Darwin's expulsion of God from the role of being a special kind of cause or designer within the whorl of natural events has been such a menacing threat for many Christians that they have often denounced the unpretentious naturalist from Downe as the source of most of the evils of late modernity. Engagement with the Darwinian depths could be a wholesome development for both faith and theology. It might lead on to larger thoughts about God: *Deus semper maior*. Pure faith, as the Song of Mary (Luke 1:46–55) expresses so exquisitely, invites us to magnify our sense of infinite mystery. Moreover, good theology, as theologian Karl Rahner has said, is always pedagogy into mystery, not a way to wrap everything up in small, digestible packets of certainty. Genuine faith is an adventure that time and again has to abandon shallow attempts to tie divine action to unperturbed order.

Theology, therefore, should amount to much more than protecting faith from a journey into depth. By and large, however, it has yet to take full advantage of evolution's abysmal and grounding challenge, and this is why a candid conversation with Darwin is good for the discipline. Theologians, Tillich would insist, should express gratitude to Darwin for bringing to our attention the fact that the idea of special creation is not needed to explain living complexity and diversity. God is not a tinkerer, designer, or first mover. God is the depth, abyss, and ground of all life and all being. As such, God relates to nature and the drama of life in a much more intimate and foundational way than through occasional interference. The scientific theory of evolution by natural selection is not a threat to the doctrine of God, only to a narrow and now defunct notion of deity and divine action.

God as Ground rather than Cause

Tillich is by no means the first religious thinker to have had such thoughts. Medieval philosophers and theologians had already begun to remove God from the lowly realm of *secondary* (natural) causes and had given to divine creativity the status of *primary* (metaphysical) cause. It is an insult to the divine infinity, they thought, to place the Creator alongside lesser causes.

Shall we then perhaps think of God as the cause of all causes? But even that is not good enough. For Tillich, talking about God as a "cause" at all is always misleading. It is the main reason for our confusion about how to think about divine action in nature and history. The category of causation does not come close to capturing what it means to say that God is Creator or that God is providentially involved in the world of finite beings. Causality is an idea that applies to the interaction of finite entities, not to that which transcends all finite things. Even "first cause" is not a large-enough idea to represent what God really is. To look for a "causal joint" between God and nature is theologically misguided and leads only to misunderstanding God's relationship to the natural world.

Nevertheless, beneath the seemingly detached scientific quest for causes lurks an unspoken, but deeply religious, concern for the depth and ground that gives being to all finite beings. Darwin's own search is no exception. At the end of the *Origin of Species*, he refers to our planet as cycling on age after age according to Newtonian laws. Darwin plants the temporally finite drama of life against the more enduring backdrop of this endless material movement. Out of the reliability of this permanent physical background, natural selection has woven on earth, for a time at least, a specter of amazing but evanescent grandeur.

When Darwin had turned decisively away from the previous habit of natural philosophers to settle scientific questions by way of theological answers, it did little to calm his own anxious sensibilities. So he had to look for other sources of confidence than those provided by his former Anglican faith or by the tepid deistic theology to which he still made occasional appeal. Could he find a foundational depth by turning to materialist philosophy? He may have been tempted to do so, but I seriously doubt that Darwin ever became the full-fledged materialist that some noted contemporary evolutionists make him out to be. And yet, there is no doubt that his ideas seemed from the beginning susceptible to being taken over by scientific naturalists, such as the German biologist Ernst Haeckel, who were already firmly committed to materialism. Even Karl Marx assumed that Darwin had gone over completely to the materialist views that were sprouting up everywhere in Europe at the time.

However, except for a few notes to himself, one does not gather the impression that Darwin's own defense against the abyss that he exposed was to fall back on the eternity of matter. Rather, I would say, his comfort came largely from the beauty and vitality of the life-world he was uncovering in a most luxuriant new way. Even though his notion of natural selection was formally mechanistic, his research almost daily led him further down into an aesthetic depth in the life-world that few others had ever come close to plumbing. Undoubtedly, the first face that evolution shows to those whose theological understanding had previously focused on design—as had Darwin's—is that of a formless abyss. But facing an abyss can be the first step toward a redemptive and healing ground that quietly reveals itself in the experience of depth.

Only by a courageous journey into the depths can one finally land on more solid ground than before. I believe that Darwin, at least tacitly, experienced what the poet Hopkins calls the "freshness deep down things." Even though he complained at times that his aesthetic sensitivities had been dulled by years of scientific research, his interest in the drama of life never abated. Again and again he landed on spiritually solid ground simply by allowing himself to be grasped by the fragile beauty of life; in this way he avoided being trapped by mind-numbing materialist notions of physical reality. Likewise, we too may find a way to connect evolution to God by way of our anticipating, as we face the future, an ever-expanding beauty in the drama of life. Undeniably, Darwin has opened up an abyss in nature, but it is one that can lead our own religious inquiry down to more solid ground beneath our naively benign impressions of nature.

Darwin, no doubt, has alerted us to depths of nature unknown throughout most of human history, and perhaps it is hard not to be distressed—at least at first—with the picture he provides of life's long struggle. One may shrink back in horror at the cruelty and waste in it all. However, like Darwin, we need not close ourselves off to the wondrous beauty that evolution has wrought, for it is ultimately in being carried away by beauty that we find ourselves truly grounded. We may ask whether the emergence of beauty is worth the tragedy that accompanies it. But consider the alternative. A world permeated by perfect design would be a world without struggle, suffering, and tragedy, but it would be a world that could never have led to intensely dramatic beauty either.

The grandeur of nature, along with the "peaceful woods and smiling fields" we view from our windows, may seem to materialist interpreters of Darwin to be a deceptive cover-up. Buried beneath surface design they see only endless ages of loss, violence, and death. But the drama has an irresistible and saving beauty to it nonetheless, especially if we locate all of it within the life of God. As we shall see in the next chapter, it is only on the mound of mortality, of dead and lost organisms and species, that the drama of life has been able to keep on playing itself out. But we need not deny that, in spite of perpetual perishing, life still goes on and carries us along with it—perhaps ultimately into the saving mystery of God.

Deep Divine Action

Finally, let me suggest that Tillich's intuition that nature has an inexhaustible dimension of depth allows theology to avoid the traps that occur whenever we wonder how God could possibly act or "intervene" in nature. Trying to figure out exactly how God influences the natural world, and especially life's evolution, too easily ends up in shallow theological speculation. Inserting divine action into a series of natural causes not only sounds silly to scientifically educated people; it also in effect reduces God to being part of nature rather than nature's abyss and ground. Thinking of God, for example, as acting in the observationally hidden domain of quantum events or in random genetic mutations ends up shrinking God's creativity down to the size of a natural cause.

Instead of seeking a crisp point of intersection between God on the one hand and a cause-and-effect series of natural events on the other, I believe the notion of nature's depth allows theology to focus instead on the more serious question of "What is *really* going on in nature?" If nature has an inexhaustible depth, we can respond to this question by differentiating reading levels, such as those of science and theology, without having to resort to fruitless speculation about how divine influence somehow "hooks itself" into natural processes.

To clarify my point, let me go back to our familiar analogy. You may read this page from the point of view of the grammatical rules that generate the sentences, or you may read it from the point of view of the ideas I am trying to get across. There is no specifiable place or series of points where the content of this page "intersects" with the grammatical rules. Rather, the expression of content or meaning on this page is distributed throughout inseparably from its grammatical underpinning. The grammatical rules are never suspended by the introduction of my message on this page, and there is no identifiable point in the grammatical structure of this page where the meaning I am trying to get across can be specifically located. However, there are different levels of depth at which we can read the same page: one level looks only at the grammar; the other looks deeper, into the meaning.

Analogously, there is no specifiable place in natural history or in life's evolution where, in order to make room for God, we have to look for an interruptive divine action that requires a suspension or special manipulation of the laws of physics, chemistry, or biology. Rather, there are different levels of depth at which we may read nature. So we may respond in a variety of ways, and at a plurality of explanatory levels, to the one question "What is really going on in nature?" or "What is really going on in the drama of life?" Nature is a physically continuous and unbroken process, but science reads events in nature at one level and theology reads the same events at another level. Each reading level leaves out content that the other includes, but there is no conflict between the two readings, even though there is often disagreement as to which reading is the more fundamental.

The important question then is not how God acts in nature, but how deep are we willing to look in our quest to understand what's *really* going on in the drama of life and the cosmos. Even within the natural sciences, there are different reading levels. At the level of physics, for example, evolution is a process of thermodynamic exchanges; but at other scientific reading levels, something else is going on. From the point of view of chemistry, evolution is a process of making and combining large molecules; from another point of view, evolution involves the transfer of information; to population geneticists, evolution is the migration of genes from one generation to the next; and so on. From the reading level of a scientifically informed Christian theology, however, evolution is an unfinished, transformative, dramatic adventure of creating and intensifying the world's freedom, consciousness, and beauty, all within the compassionate life of the triune God. The fact that nature has an inexhaustible depth allows both science and theology to comment on the drama of life without coming into conflict with each other.

Chapter 8

Death

It has always appeared to me more satisfactory to look at the immense amount of pain & suffering in this world, as the inevitable result of the natural sequence of events, i.e., general laws, rather than from the direct intervention of God.
—Charles Darwin, Letter to Mary Boole, 1866[1]

The last enemy to be destroyed is death.
—the apostle Paul, in 1 Corinthians 15:26

Promise the earth a hundred million more years of continued growth. If, at the end of that period, it is evident that the whole of conscious-ness must revert to zero, without its secret essence being garnered anywhere at all, then, I insist, we shall lay down our arms—and man-kind will be on strike. The prospect of a total death (and that is a word to which we should devote much thought if we are to gauge its destructive effect on our souls) will, I warn you, when it has become part of our consciousness, immediately dry up in us the springs from which our efforts are drawn.
—Teilhard de Chardin[2]

*E*volution has produced a stupendous display of diversity, innumerable spe-cies of life, multiple modes of sentience, and recently the human capacity for self-awareness. However, the drama of life on earth has featured at least five massive extinctions as well, and on a smaller scale the evolutionary story is one in which every living, sentient, and conscious organism eventually dies. From all appearances, if evolution is a drama, it is a tragic one. Every organic actor in the production called "life" eventually perishes and becomes interred in the irretrievable past. All living beings are eventually lost and forgotten. In the long run, nothing in the universe is forever, and physics informs us that the universe as a whole will not last indefinitely either.

The fragility of life is especially troubling. Living organisms flourish for a season at best, and then they vanish. New birth is inseparable from the mortality that opens up a space for it. In the meantime, however, the life-story keeps going on in a continuous and unbroken way. Individual organisms disappear, but every one of them contributes to a trail of events that, as we can see clearly after Darwin, accumulates into a most intriguing set of outcomes, not the least of which is the human species. Without the death of individual living beings in each new generation, the story of life would never have gone far and would even have come to a dead end. Organisms, if they were immortal, would have piled up on one another, and the countless variations needed by natural selection to fashion new species would be limited for lack of space. Evolution relies on variation and selection if it is to make any advances in complexity and diversity. But variation, as Darwin came to realize, needs to be abundant if it is to produce even a few accidentally adaptive forms. Thus it requires an enormous spread of *time*, and along with ample time it stipulates the death of every present generation of living beings. Without death, evolution could not be truly inventive. If a sufficient supply of variations is to become available for selection, death is a necessity, not a riddle to fret over.

So even though death is an agonizing puzzle to most human beings and their religious faiths, a purely naturalistic method of inquiry after Darwin can find an intelligible place for it in the total scheme of life. Just as suffering makes natural sense as an evolutionary adaptation in sentient beings (helping them survive by warning them of impending harm or fatality), so death seems to make sense as part of the overall evolution of living diversity. Death and suffering are both essential to the survival of populations of genes as they flow from one generation to the next. Why bother then to look for a theological meaning to suffering or death? Hasn't Darwin's science in company with the field of genetics taken us as far into the depth of life, suffering, and death as the human mind can possibly reach?

To evolutionary naturalists, death seems to make good sense scientifically, even though it is no less personally agonizing to them than to anyone else. It is essential to Christianity, however, *not* to tolerate any intelligible place for death and suffering, at least in the larger setting of being. Christianity is about the eventual wiping away of all tears by God, the final release from suffering, and the ultimate defeat of death through the resurrection of Christ. So what sense can Christian theology make of the riddle of evolutionary extinction and the demise of every organism? How can Christians pronounce life to be good, as God does in Genesis, if death, along with so much struggle and pain in sentient beings, is so integral to the creative process? To Darwin, evolution seemed increasingly godless the deeper he saw into the enormity of suffering, struggle, and death that are part of it. Yes, something grand had come into existence as a result of births, deaths, variation, natural selection, and deep time; but can one plausibly connect nature to the purposes of a beneficent deity after looking directly at how evolution relies so heavily on death?

Along with Darwin, many evolutionists today deny that there can be a persuasive theological answer to this question. However, unlike scientific naturalism, it is the task of Christian theology to make it clear that death has no intelligible place in the total—and dramatically speaking, that means the "final"—scheme of things. It is theologically inappropriate to look for a rationally acceptable place for death in God's creation. Doing so would give death a legitimacy that might lead us to tolerate and even justify it here and now rather than taking it as an evil to be fought against and overcome. It is not the job of theology to justify death by situating it solely within the context of a purely naturalistic understanding of the universe. Instead, theology asks whether the naturalistic point of view as such is intelligible.

It is not. Evolutionary naturalism has no reasonable answer to the question of why there is anything at all rather than nothing, or why the universe is intelligible at all, or why the universe is the blend of contingency, law, and time, which gives it a narrative character that in turn allows life to evolve in the dramatic way it does. Evolutionary naturalism has no answer to these questions other than to say, "This is just the way things happen to be." Theologically speaking, this naturalistic answer is unacceptable since it amounts to saying that our search for intelligibility will ultimately meet up with final absurdity. This is hardly a prediction that can sustain an endless, ongoing search for understanding. Scientists themselves should take no comfort in a vision of reality that perches the natural world on the pedestal of final unintelligibility. Theology, on the other hand, because of its insistence that nature must be ultimately rooted in a transcendent ground of intelligibility, goodness, beauty, and truth, turns out to be a much better friend and supporter of scientific inquiry than evolutionary naturalism could ever be.

Theology is critical of evolutionary naturalism most of all, however, because the latter makes such an easy settlement with death. Even though death may be intelligible to science as part of nature, nature itself remains unintelligible to theology when considered apart from its eternal ground and depth. Consequently, the present chapter makes no attempt to make sense of death by staying within the cramped confines of a naturalistic worldview. Instead, it looks for a way to understand the Christian hope for redemption from, and final victory over, death in a post-Darwinian age. To do so, however, it does not in any way challenge evolutionary science, only evolutionary naturalism.

A Wider Vision

To Christian theologians, the challenge after Darwin is to think of the universe as a place of promise and purpose *in spite of* the fact that everything in the life-story—and eventually the universe itself—fades into oblivion. Life, it is clear, is not an unmixed good, especially since it is all subject to death. Is it possible then to arrive at a plausible theological understanding of death that does not contradict evolutionary science, but that takes us deeper into the drama of life and the universe than science alone can?

I believe our theological conversation with Darwin may be considerably broadened and enriched at this point by considering several ideas of the philosopher and religious thinker Alfred North Whitehead (1861–1947). I shall not give a full account of Whitehead's thought or defend every aspect of it here. Instead, I shall focus on what he has to say about the general fact of nature's *perishability*, of which the death of living organisms is the most troubling kind.

Whitehead observes that the fact of evil in the natural world comes down, in the end, to the plain and simple fact that things perish. The naked fact of perishing is the fundamental issue that religions, philosophies, and theologies have always had to address. Organic death is the major instance of a larger enigma: why does anything in nature perish at all? Perishing as such is the problem, and what bothers us in a special way about the death of every sentient being is that a center of experience—in other words, a *subject*—apparently disappears for good. Nowhere is this dissolution more agonizing than when the mind of a loved one disintegrates or a formerly healthy person suddenly lapses into a vegetative state and then finally into death. However, theology must connect even these most disquieting examples of decomposition to the more general fact that *nothing* in nature lasts forever.

As each new moment arrives in the flow of time, the present moment is thrust into the past. There it eventually is lost, at least to human memory. It is this fading of every present pulse of actuality into the forgotten past that constitutes the "ultimate evil in the temporal world." "The world," as Whitehead puts it, "is haunted by terror at the loss of the past, with its familiarities and its loved ones. It seeks escape from time in its character of 'perpetually perishing.'"[3] When things perish, it is the loss of immediacy that evokes the kind of anguished concern to which religions have tried, in diverse ways, to apply some measure of consolation. Theology, therefore, needs to situate our uneasiness about the perpetual dying that goes on in evolution within the wider fact that all finite things perish.

Theologian Paul Tillich, whom we met in the previous chapter, conjectures that beneath our human anxiety about death lies a more fundamental concern, that of being forgotten forever. As the present is being pushed into the past and then becomes lost to human memory, we worry that we too shall eventually be forgotten. The anxiety of having to die, and indirectly our sensitivity to the fact that every organism is mortal, is the "anxiety of being eternally forgotten."[4] This is why people of all times and places have sought, through a variety of ways, to ensure that they will be remembered:

> The Greeks spoke of glory as the conquest of being forgotten. Today, the same thing is called "historical significance." If one can, one builds memorial foundations. It is consoling to think that we might be remembered for a certain time beyond death not only by those who loved us or hated us or admired us, but also by those who never knew us except now by name. Some names are remembered for centuries. Hope is expressed in the poet's proud assertion that "the traces of his earthly days cannot vanish in eons." But those traces, which unquestionably exist in the physical world, are not we ourselves, and they don't bear our name. They do not keep us from being forgotten.[5]

So, if Tillich and Whitehead are correct, unless there exists beneath the abyss of death a ground of permanence that can redeem *all* perishing, we would have to conclude that evil is finally victorious. And if the evolutionary drama is to make *final* sense, then somehow the dissolution of even the most trivial instances of life cannot be absolute. If redemption is a realistic possibility, the series of events that make up the life-story and the larger universe must flow into the bosom of an everlasting compassion that saves it all from final nothingness and that rescues it from eventual incoherence. Deeper than evolution, if evolution is to escape final absurdity, there must be something that gathers up, and holds in eternal memory, the stream of events that make up the drama of life and the cosmic process as a whole.

Can theology justifiably remain confident, in the age of science, that the obvious perishing in the world-process is not the final word, and that a repository of permanence—in other words, something everlasting—saves the world from utter loss and ultimate unintelligibility? The intuition of many faith traditions, including Christianity, is that an unshakable ground of timeless eternity endures in the depths of nature and history. It is this eternity, at least to those who are sensitive to it, that redeems all perishing, and it is especially in our religions that we become aware of this dimension of intransience. Religion, as Whitehead has put it in very general terms,

> is the vision of something which stands beyond, behind, and within, the passing flux of immediate things; something which is real, and yet waiting to be realized; something which is a remote possibility, and yet the greatest of present facts; something that gives meaning to all that passes, and yet eludes apprehension; something whose possession is the final good, and yet is beyond all reach; something which is the ultimate ideal, and the hopeless quest.[6]

But is the religious intuition of a permanence behind and within the flow of perishing moments anything more than an illusion? Perhaps a glimpse of one possible response can be found in an intriguing couplet coined by the skeptic and poet Arthur Hugh Clough:

> It fortifies my soul to know,
> That though I perish truth is so.

Even though I will perish, as will everything else in cosmic process, in life's evolution, and in human history, nevertheless the *fact* that I have existed at all, even if only for a brief time, is imperishable. In evolution, countless organisms have perished in several major extinctions, but the *fact* that living beings existed at all in each epoch will never perish. It is as true today as it was 200 million years ago, for example, that dinosaurs existed. Trillions of years from now, after the big bang universe has died of cold, and all of life along with it, it will even then be true that dinosaurs had lived for millions of years on earth. Nothing will ever have obliterated the *truth* that dinosaurs and you and I had existed.

But *where* will this be true, and to what or to whom? Charles Hartshorne, an American philosopher greatly influenced by Whitehead, considers this to be an important question. He acknowledges that "there was once no such individual as myself, even as something that was 'going to exist.' But centuries after my death, there will have been that very individual which I am."[7] In other words, it will *forever* be true that I have existed, along with dinosaurs and other extinct forms of life. But, again, where will this be true forever? What is it that will register everlastingly the truth that dinosaurs and you and I had lived? For Hartshorne—and indeed for Christian theology as well—it is the eternity of God.

Deeper than evolution, beneath all becoming, perishing, and death, Christians believe, there abides an eternal repository that retains with full immediacy every event that ever happens, including the whole drama of life. Behind and within all that ever occurs in the story of the universe, there is a "tender care that nothing be lost," as Whitehead puts it.[8] It is this principle of care that prevents the absolute erasure of the record of events in evolution and the emergent universe. Only the reality of a saving, compassionate, providential permanence could ever respond adequately to the questions that arise from our evolutionary awareness of extinction and death in the drama of life.

However, Darwin and evolutionary naturalists would surely ask whether it is realistic to suppose, in the midst of our experience of perpetual perishing, that the cosmic past can somehow endure everlastingly, even though most of it lies beyond human memory. Whitehead and Hartshorne claim that it is indeed realistic as long as we realize that nature is a process of becoming composed of events, occasions, or happenings, and not material chunks of stuff. For if the universe is made up of transient events, as contemporary physics now also realizes, it is their very perishing that allows the past moments to accumulate and have an abiding influence on the present. And, I would add, it is the perishing of each present moment that also allows the future to keep arriving on the frontier of every new present. In evolution, it is the openness of every past and present event to being synthesized into a new future that allows the drama of life to keep going on.

Theologically speaking, if the evolving cosmos is to escape the abyss of final nothingness, there must be something that receives the whole story into itself and saves it all with unfading immediacy. The Christian idea of God points to such a reality. The compassion of God, as Christians are encouraged by the promises of the prophets and Jesus to believe, exists faithfully and forever. A theology of evolution extends the Christian vision of divine fidelity into the depths of nature and evolution. Only an everlasting fidelity distinct from, but deeply related to, the universe itself could truly redress the fact of perpetual perishing. Furthermore, since in human beings the universe has been lifted to an unprecedented intensity of awareness (at least on earth), and evolution has now become conscious of itself, it is inconceivable that any truly cosmic redemption would tolerate the final snuffing out of the very consciousness to which the natural world has been straining so long to give birth. Our hope for conscious, subjective survival of death makes very good sense if the universe and evolution have an everlasting importance to God.

The Limits of Science

Needless to say, any sort of scientific proof of this theological proposal is out of the question. For the Christian, everything I have proposed here is a matter of hope, not scientific certainty. The power of God to redeem all of life from death can be justified not by intellectual effort but only by trust in the love and fidelity of God as made manifest in Jesus Christ. But if, as Jesus promised, the hairs of our head are numbered, and if, as the psalmist earlier proclaimed, all our tears flow into God's flask (Ps. 56:8), then somehow every perishing life and every past event is preserved eternally in God.

Paul Tillich expresses this religious intuition in a more classical way than does Whitehead:

> Nothing in the universe is unknown, nothing real is ultimately forgotten. The atom that moves in an immeasurable path today and the atom that moved in an immeasurable path billions of years ago are rooted in the eternal ground. There is no absolute, no completely forgotten past, because the past, like the future, is rooted in the divine life. Nothing is completely pushed into the past. Nothing real is absolutely lost and forgotten.[9]

Whitehead would add that in God's experience, the cumulative series of cosmic events and experiences never fades. Each instance of life that perishes in the context of our own limited experience, or that goes extinct during an epoch of evolution, dwells forever in God without loss. God is the underlying permanence that fully preserves everything that occurs in the entire cosmic process.[10] From our own transient perspective, each momentary event eventually drifts into the past, where it is eventually forgotten, but it still remains in the divine memory with lasting intensity.

Again, we cannot prove any of this scientifically, nor should we even want to do so, given the limitations of scientific method. Nevertheless, science has stretched our awareness of the extent of perishing that occurs in evolution, and so it demands a corresponding enlargement of our sense of God and divine compassion. Consequently, Christian hope after Darwin assumes the reality of a God large and generous enough to embrace the entire drama of life and the cosmos, into which the evolution of life is intricately woven.

Whitehead's understanding of religion in the age of evolution necessitates such an expansiveness in our understanding of God. In this philosopher's understanding, God is that which stands beyond, behind, and within the passing flux of immediate things, rescuing whatever may seem from our own vantage point to be "utter final wreck and tragedy." God "saves the world as it passes into the immediacy of his own experience."[11] In a world conceived of as a temporal process, each experience adds something new, by way of contrast, to the divine experience. Every perishing event and every death of every organism is eternally redeemed by its "relation to the completed whole."[12] Taken into the endless breadth of the ever-intensifying beauty that we may call God, evolution and the universe from which life emerges are endowed with imperishable value and meaning.[13]

Each life is invited to participate in and contribute itself to this wider beauty. For human beings, this self-contribution is symbolized especially in acts of worship. In a most intimate way, my entire existence, vitality, and subjectivity are, in the act of worship, made available to be synthesized into the transformative world process and ultimately into the life of God. My personal existence is still continuous with cosmic beginnings and is everlastingly so. For even after the cosmos eventually dissolves, the story of its having been will still be true—preserved forever in God's saving memory. Accordingly, the question of who I am, how I came to emerge from the universe, and whether I can be redeemed from absolute perishing—all this is inescapably bound up with the universe and its final destiny. In a communal setting, religious worship symbolizes my grateful consent to contribute my life and efforts to this everlastingly significant cosmic drama.

The idea that the *whole* scheme of perishing things can be saved in God's transforming love may be easier to grasp if we learn to think, along with Whitehead, that at its most elemental level, the universe is made up not of spatially measurable bits of matter but of temporal events, occasions, or happenings. The problem with thinking of the elemental cosmic components simply as physical units, as materialists usually do, is that these spatialized bits of stuff eventually dissolve and disappear. Events, on the other hand, have the quality of being able to keep adding up into a continuous series in which what goes before is never completely lost. Material entities disintegrate, but events accumulate. Whitehead and Hartshorne emphasize that the cosmos is a cumulative temporal series of events, not just a collection of things hanging around in space. Modern scientific materialism, on the contrary—especially in its mechanistic portraits of nature—has unfortunately rigidified nature by trying to fit it fully into spatially measurable models. But in their most concrete actuality, both the evolution of life and the larger cosmic process—as a more up-to-date physics also allows—consist of narrative happenings, not bits of matter. The totality of events in nature gathers itself into an unbroken drama, one that theology may think of as being taken forever into the life of God.

The Hiddenness of God

Still, with the Darwinian skeptics we can only wonder why the God who promises deliverance of all beings from absolute perishing remains so hidden and seemingly far off as deaths keep mounting up in evolution. Why does what Whitehead calls "the final good" and "the ultimate ideal" remain beyond all reach? Why does "that which gives meaning to all that passes" always elude present apprehension? Science by itself can make no sense of what lies hidden "beyond, behind, and within" the flux of natural and historical events. It insists on clarity here and now since it can base its predictions only on what is presently available to empirical inquiry. Can theology make better sense of it all?

Theology may at least point out that the hiddenness of God to conscious beings here and now is consistent with the fact that the universe is still coming into being.[14] Religious expectation or hope, though quite distinct from science, is logically compatible with the fact that we humans are part of an immense cosmos still in the making. An undeniable implication of science today is that we live in a still-unfinished universe. If our universe were completely finalized here and now, we could justifiably insist on absolute clarity. However, as long as the world is still being created, and as long as the drama of life has yet to be concluded, we cannot reasonably expect here and now to make out clearly what it is all about, or what lies beyond, behind, and within it. We have to wait.

For this reason it is not unexpected that what Whitehead calls the greatest of present facts—in other words, God—must remain beyond our grasp. An unfinished universe is one in which awareness of God comes only in the mode of promise rather than conclusive comprehension. The religious intuition of a divine permanence beyond, behind, within—or beneath—the passing flux of immediate things can take hold of us only if we are willing to sacrifice our longing for present clarity and allow our hearts and minds to be suffused with patient and long-suffering hope.

Chapter 9

Duty

The following proposition seems to me in a high degree probable—namely, that any animal whatever, endowed with well-marked social instincts, the parental and filial affections being here included, would inevitably acquire a moral sense or conscience, as soon as its intellectual powers had become as well, or nearly as well developed, as in man.

If... men were reared under precisely the same conditions as hive-bees, there can hardly be a doubt that our unmarried females would, like the worker-bees, think it a sacred duty to kill their brothers, and mothers would strive to kill their fertile daughters; and no one would think of interfering.

—*Charles Darwin,* The Descent of Man, *1871*[1]

According to the great philosopher Immanuel Kant (1724–1804), thoughtful and responsible people need to ask three big questions: What can I know? What ought I do? What may I hope? Kant assumed that there is some connection between knowledge on the one hand and hope and duty on the other. Still, he could never have foreknown the extent to which scientific knowledge, especially evolutionary biology, would challenge human assumptions about what we can realistically know and hope for and what we should be doing, morally speaking, with our lives.

Kant was especially intrigued by the fact that for the most part, human beings have a sense of duty, morality, or obligation. Why do we? Along with classical theology, he assumed that each of us has an innate moral sense imprinted on our souls by God. For Kant, "the moral law within" is better evidence of the existence of God than anything else philosophy could discover, even though "the starry skies above" are certainly a source of religious wonder as well. So the duty-obsessed Kant could never have anticipated how the Darwinian revolution is now leading many educated people today to the belief that moral awareness is fixed in our minds and hearts not by God, but instead by evolutionary causes.

Darwin was vaguely familiar with Kant, having been persuaded by a learned acquaintance to read the philosopher's *Metaphysic of Ethics*. After doing so he commented:

> It has interested me much to see how differently two men may look at the same points, though I fully feel how presumptuous it sounds to put myself even for a moment in the same bracket with Kant;—the one man a great philosopher looking exclusively into his own mind, the other a degraded wretch looking from the outside thro' apes & savages at the moral sense of mankind.[2]

At least here, Darwin allows that the remarkable fact of moral sensitivity admits of different levels of understanding. But for many evolutionary naturalists today, it seems self-evident that our sense of duty is simply an adaptation, a product of selfish genes, *rather than* a mark of our existing in the presence of an infinite goodness that places moral demands upon us. Instead of having descended vertically from God on high, hasn't our sense of duty emerged horizontally, in the Darwinian sense of descent, from an evolutionary past in which competition, struggle, and adaptation are the real sculptors of our behavioral repertoire? And isn't it likely that a few ancestral hordes of hominids, and later anatomically modern human beings, eventually adapted, survived, and reproduced only because they just happened to carry genes that programmed them to live cooperatively together?

In other words, don't genes for decent social behavior and even altruism exist in us today only because we have inherited tendencies that have promoted human gene propagation in the past? Haven't we survived as a species not because our consciences are attracted to a transcendent goodness, and not because of any tacit intuition of a divine command, but simply because, in the struggle to adapt, genes that make us dutiful have won out over those that do not? An increasing number of Darwinians today are answering "yes" to these questions.

Darwin, after writing the *Origin of Species*, became increasingly preoccupied with the question of how moral behavior originated and developed during human evolution. His *Descent of Man* dealt explicitly with this issue along with the larger question of human origins, a topic that he had not formally addressed in the earlier book. In the *Descent of Man* (1871), the second most important of his major writings, Darwin asks how our species came to evolve gradually out of its prehuman ancestry. This inquiry, Darwin realized, is deeply entangled with the question of how the distinctively human sense of moral obligation arose and developed. For among the attributes that might seem to set us apart amid the vast array of living species on earth is our often rigorous devotion to duty and, more fundamentally, the moral passions from which our ethical imperatives seem to arise. Human religious tendencies also make us distinct, certainly, and I shall have more to say about these and their linkage to morality in the next chapter. Likewise our heightened capacity for reflective self-awareness differentiates human mental life from that of other species. In this chapter, however, it is the human sense of duty that we need to examine anew after Darwin.

We may begin this all-too-brief deliberation by remembering again that, according to Darwin, some organisms win and others lose out in the struggle for existence. Those that have a higher probability of surviving and reproducing are called "fit," and the losers are regarded as "unfit." However, scientists today agree that there is more than competition going on in adaptive evolution. Darwin himself was aware that fitness requires cooperation and not just competition among the members of a group or species, as well as among different species; but biologists today see even more clearly than Darwin that evolution is just as much a matter of cooperation as of competition. Even "altruism"—by which evolutionists today mean an organism's sacrificing itself and its own opportunities for reproductive success for the sake of the survival of the larger set of genes shared with one's kin—occurs abundantly in the story of life on earth.

Most Christians, along with Kant, assume that altruism is the noblest human expression of "virtue," but contemporary evolutionists have been increasingly amazed by the degree of altruism and other kinds of cooperation in nonhuman species as well. If altruism is the supreme example of morality, then it seems to have been going on long before human beings appeared on earth. The birth of morality, many Darwinians now claim, occurred as part of a purely natural process by which genes get passed along from one generation to the next.[3] Darwin, we recognize, knew nothing about genes, but today's evolutionists do; many of them have concluded that natural selection works not so much to ensure the survival of the fittest individual organisms but instead to preserve the most adaptive sets of shared genes that allow a group or species to survive and reproduce.

What is the meaning of this shift of perspective from individual organisms to gene populations as far as explaining our own sense of duty is concerned? For an increasing number of evolutionary naturalists, what it all means is that our own inclination to be cooperative and altruistic has been programmed into us by segments of DNA, *not* by God. It means that if there is a genetic basis to ethics, the Kantian postulate that our sense of duty is rooted in an intuition of a divine set of imperatives is no longer a necessary explanation. More than likely Darwin himself, if he were alive today, would adopt this new account of human ethical instincts. He would be intrigued by today's gene's-eye biological perspective, according to which "altruism" has the technical and somewhat restrictive meaning of putting one's own genetic future at risk so that the larger population of genes shared with one's kin may survive. Today this is called "kin selection."

Suppose, for example, that a young prairie dog just happens to possess a more altruistic set of genes than its siblings or kin. If so, it is more likely than its relatives to stick its neck out of its hole and warn the others when a predator is near. It also stands a greater chance of being eaten up as a result of this audacity. But even though that unfortunate prairie dog turns out to be "unfit" in the original Darwinian sense (because it no longer has any chance of surviving and reproducing), its altruistic warning gives its kin and their genes a better chance of surviving. Consequently, even though the heroic individual member of a species leaves no offspring, the whole pool of the genes it shares with its kin, including genes for cooperation and altruism, can still be passed on to future generations. This is known as *inclusive* fitness.

Can Darwin Explain Duty?

Many biologists and philosophers now therefore insist that gene survival, in which segments of DNA "strive" to replicate themselves across many generations, is the ultimate reason why we too cooperate and make sacrifices and, generally speaking, behave ourselves. Not surprisingly, they also agree that after Darwin and Mendel, there is no longer any need for a theological explanation or justification of morality. Now that gene-savvy evolutionary biology can explain our inborn aptitude for moral behavior, what could theology possibly have to add? Maybe Kant can be forgiven for thinking that only the existence of God can ground the unconditional character of the call of conscience, but science now has a simpler explanation: gene survival. Cultural factors also shape the content of morality, as Darwin and Dawkins both acknowledge, but ultimately our tendency to act morally, and especially altruistically, is a matter of adaptation, a topic for biology rather than theology.

Furthermore, if a neo-Darwinian explanation of altruism is sufficiently illuminating, one may assume that there is no such thing as exceptional virtue or real moral heroism either. Morality is a by-product of genetic determinism, and so the belief that our actions are rooted in an underlying freedom, courage, loftiness of character, or personal integrity is an illusion. Christian charity, from an evolutionary perspective, is no less a product of gene survival than is the lone prairie dog's self-sacrifice. This is a religiously startling idea since the capacity to sacrifice oneself freely out of love for another is a quality that Christianity has associated with the highest degree of moral existence. Christian theology has even insisted that exceptional expressions of love require a special influx of divine grace. It has taught that self-sacrificial love is a supernatural virtue—or else it would be more commonplace.

Nowadays many Darwinians point out, however, that altruism emerged much earlier in evolution than the human species did. It is already evident in the "cooperation" required for at least some species to last for many generations. Worker ants, for example, do not pass on their own genes, but in the context of their complex social setting, their self-sacrificial activity promotes the reproductive success of the whole commune. Worker ants serve the good of the whole colony even though they are not involved directly in reproducing their own genes.[4] Biologists can now point to many other examples of such edifying altruism in the animal kingdom.

Cooperation also exists among nonkin as well as between and among different species. This kind of cooperation is known as "reciprocal altruism," a purely natural set of interactions in which one organism benefits another, and thus enhances the latter's reproductive opportunities, with the implicit expectation that the favor will be returned. There is no need to discuss the notion of reciprocal altruism any further here except to point out that it implies once again that self-sacrificial behavior can be accounted for apparently without reference to divine inspiration. Morality, therefore, seems more natural and less supernatural than ever to scientifically minded people today. Even expressions of charity that Christians consider to be the epitome of virtuous behavior are taken to be nothing more than a consequence of the blind drive that populations of genes must possess in order to achieve reproductive success. Many Darwinians now wonder whether even the most heroic lives and acts of self-sacrifice amount to anything more than the inevitable outcome of impersonal natural selection.

If so, then the human sense of duty no longer needs the support of a theological worldview. We can satisfactorily account for our moral habits by the fact that altruistic human genes have been more reproductively successful than uncooperative ones. Moreover, it would seem that evolution handily explains our moral failures as well. Immoral acts and inclinations are simply vestiges of the untamed instinctual endowment we have inherited from our animal past.[5]

In any case, the moral inclinations that lead us to cooperate with one another do not point to a Kantian deity or a Platonic heaven. To many evolutionary naturalists, the very idea of an eternal goodness by which we might measure our conduct is itself a fiction devised unconsciously by our brains to assist the process of gene propagation. So, although we may think (mistakenly) that our moral lives somehow reflect the transcendent goodness of God, our allegedly exceptional acts of virtue are natural, not supernatural. They are consequences of a purely physical process of events that can be illuminated best by a gene-centered biology.

This is only a sketch of how contemporary evolutionary accounts of morality go, but for the purposes of this chapter, it should suffice. I simply want to drive home the point that a good number of evolutionary thinkers are now convinced that, after Darwin, morality does not need the support of faith or theology since it can be explained more tidily in a purely natural way. Furthermore, as the next chapter shows, these same evolutionists claim that religion also is ultimately a concoction devised by blind biological processes to support the moral instincts necessary for gene survival. They take religion's promises of heavenly reward and threats of hell's punishment to be illusions that persuade us to cooperate and practice altruism by causing us to think (again mistakenly) that our moral imperatives have been stamped directly by God on stone tablets and human hearts. Consequently, now that science has developed a purely natural and more economical explanation of our inclination to be virtuous, we can dispense with religion and theology altogether. They are not necessary to explain our sense of duty or justify even our noblest ethical precepts.

Are Evolutionary Accounts of Morality Coherent?

However, a serious theological conversation with Darwin will expose evolutionary accounts of duty and virtue as insufficient. And if such accounts are taken to be the ultimate explanation of our moral intuitions or instincts, they can even be shown to be self-contradictory. I allow here that evolutionary stories about the gradual development of a moral sense among humans may be interesting and even illuminating. Darwinian accounts of the gradual emergence of morality may be accurate as far as they go. The arrival of moral sensitivity and ethical codes, after all, is a significant development in the larger drama of life, and so evolutionary scientists have every reason to trace morality's origins and development in the setting of natural history. However, Darwinian biology cannot, in a truly foundational way, account for our attraction to goodness any more than a study of the gradual evolution of the human mind can account fully for our attraction to truth. Nor can evolutionary science justify what Kant rightly recognized to be the unconditional character of the call to duty.

To drive home this point, I want to make four observations. First, the evolutionary naturalists are themselves attracted to moral ideals or values such as honesty, truth seeking, overcoming ignorance (such as religious belief), and promoting science education. Second, the same evolutionists take these lofty values to be absolute, unconditional, and inviolable. They even become morally outraged when others fail to respect what they take to be the "rightness" of their own commitment to these values. Third, however, their commitment to these values could not function to guide their own moral conduct if their attraction to honesty, truth, and scientific integrity were consistently understood to be nothing more at bottom than an evolutionary adaptation. And fourth, even if natural selection is able to shed light on immature stages of moral development, this does not mean that it can fully explain each and every expression of our moral life. Let us now look more closely at each of these four points.

1. Evolutionary naturalists are themselves attracted to moral ideals and ethical values. For example, Richard Dawkins and Daniel Dennett dutifully abide by what has been called the "ethic of knowledge." They adhere passionately to the belief that scientific knowing is the only morally right way to put our minds in touch with truth, and they cast scorn on anyone who refuses to accept their exacting standards of ethical existence. Evolutionary naturalism, as it turns out, is rooted in a profoundly ethical belief system where the practice of virtue is essential to appropriate knowing.

Long before Dawkins and Dennett came along, the renowned biochemist Jacques Monod had already called upon his readers to embrace the "ethic of knowledge."[6] The starting point of ethical existence is what he called the postulate of objectivity, by which he meant that only the detached kind of knowledge that scientific method employs is ethically permitted in the project of seeking truth.[7] Even earlier (1877), the philosopher W. K. Clifford had also promoted an ethic of knowledge when he declared: "It is wrong always, everywhere, and for anyone, to believe anything upon insufficient evidence."[8]

If you have ever read Dawkins or Dennett, you cannot miss the ethical idealism that underlies their work as well. A passionate sense of duty to their fellow humans leads them to reprimand those of us who still wallow irresponsibly in the illusions of religious faith. Their own ethic of knowledge is almost puritanical in its categorical demand that responsible people *must* detach themselves from theological ways of understanding and knowing.

Such detachment, they preach, demands an ethical asceticism to which weak and lazy-minded religious believers fail to aim.

2. Evolutionary naturalists such as Dennett and Dawkins take for granted that the values and moral imperatives surrounding their ethic of knowledge are absolute. Truth seeking and academic honesty, they insist, cannot be looked upon as merely arbitrary ethical standards, created ad hoc by certain individuals or human communities at certain places geographically, or at limited times in history. Rather, the ethic of knowledge is binding categorically on all people at all times from now on. If the ethic of knowledge were merely my own concoction, then I would be permitted to give it only relative rather than absolute respect. I could say that I have decided that truth seeking by way of scientific method is not an important, let alone an absolute, value for me. However, it is hard to imagine that any serious evolutionary naturalist would tolerate such moral relativism.

Only an unwavering moral commitment to ethical values that they take to be *unconditionally* good could ever motivate evolutionary naturalists to spend so much energy promoting the ethic of knowledge in order to make the world better, at least as they understand "better." Their moral injunction to use science as the measuring rod or criterion of right knowing is unbending. In pursuit of what they take to be the highest value of all, objective knowing, they are resolute that following the method of science is *absolutely* imperative.

Nevertheless, we may ask what it is that makes this commandment absolute or unconditional. Since evolutionary naturalists deny the existence of God, and therefore any eternal or universal reason why we should follow any moral imperatives at all, including the postulate of objectivity, what ground are they standing on when they issue the decree that we *must* submit to their ethic of knowledge? The evolutionary naturalist will simply reply, without saying why, that it is "just wrong" to allow ourselves to be seduced by nonscientific ways of thinking, especially religious faith and theology. But is this reply enough to establish the absolute inviolability of the ethic of knowledge?

3. The evolutionary naturalists' uncompromising commitment to the values associated with the ethic of knowledge—honesty, truth, and scientific integrity—could not function to guide their own moral conduct if their attraction to these values were consistently understood to be nothing more at bottom than an evolutionary adaptation. For if the roots of all human ethical instincts are ultimately biological, as evolutionary naturalists explicitly claim, then isn't the ethic of knowledge itself nothing more than a product of blind natural selection? And if so, how can it be taken as absolute and unconditional? Why can't it be explained away like every other ethical imperative as ultimately nothing more than the unintentional result of selective pressures on gene populations?

Why, indeed, should I take any moral imperative seriously if adaptation is ultimately all there is to it? As long as evolutionists maintain that our sense of moral ideals can be explained *ultimately* as a trick played on us by our genes, it will be quite hard for the same evolutionists to justify the absolute seriousness with which they themselves make the moral claim that honesty and truth seeking are unconditional moral values, to which we must all bow.

Here the self-contradiction in evolutionary naturalism is blatant. Why am I obliged to obey their ethic of knowledge if, like all other ethical demands, this set of imperatives is ultimately rooted in the mindless impetuosity of genes to get into the next generation? Although some evolutionary naturalists allow that cultural influences also have something to do with the formation of ethical imperatives, there is nothing in these historically and socially conditioned factors that can render any ethical directives absolute and unconditional either. If evolutionary and/or cultural influences were the only determinants of my sense of duty, then why should I bother to be ethical at all? And in particular, why should I submit to the evolutionary naturalist's ethic of knowledge if every inclination to duty is ultimately reducible to a biological adaptation?

A purely evolutionary explanation of virtue, I am arguing, cannot justify taking seriously the evolutionary naturalist's own highest ethical ideal, that of seeking truth for truth's sake. So, even for the evolutionary naturalist, morality and virtue are not really being fully accounted for ultimately in evolutionary terms after all. This raises an important question: What plausible justification is there, if any, for the evolutionary naturalist's fervent and unconditional commitment to honesty and truth? If evolutionary adaptation is not a sufficient justification of the moral absoluteness of the ethic of knowledge, then what is? For the evolutionary naturalist, it cannot be God since God doesn't exist. Is it perhaps cultural conditioning? Or is morality ultimately a purely human creation?

In response to such questions, Dawkins, Coyne, Gould, and some other evolutionary naturalists, almost in a state of embarrassment, abruptly break off any real connection to Darwin at this point. They agree that Darwinian biology cannot specify the *content* of human moral life. They would actually agree that even to try to derive human moral principles directly from evolutionary biology is itself immoral, especially since deliberate attempts to imitate natural selection in our relationship with other humans and other living beings violates every standard of fairness and compassion. The survival of the fittest is hardly a respectable model for decent social interaction. So where do our hard-core evolutionists go to find a justification for the absolute and unconditional character of their most important ethical commitments?

As far as I can tell from reading Dawkins, Coyne, and Gould, they all give the same answer: it is "up to us" to decide what is and what is not morally binding. Neither theology nor adaptive evolution is an acceptable guide, ethically speaking; therefore, only human beings, either on their own or in community with others, are left to decide what is right or wrong. I wish I could find a more nuanced response to the question of how these evolutionary naturalists justify the uncompromising quality of moral imperatives such as their postulate to be scientifically objective. However, Dawkins, Coyne, and Gould leave us to fall back only on "our own" moral discretion since there can never be a purely Darwinian derivation of moral imperatives. I'll have to leave it up to the reader to decide whether leaving the creation of moral meaning and values up to us is the best we can do in our attempts to place ethical existence on a firm foundation in the age of evolution.

Other evolutionists, as we have seen, are not so eager to abandon Darwin when it comes to explaining why we are moral beings. If we are to take Darwin seriously, they believe, natural selection must then be the *ultimate* explanation of everything living, including our moral instincts. It must be the ultimate explanation of the ethic of knowledge as well as all other moral aspirations. However, even if there is an evolutionary explanation of how our moral instincts came to be part of human existence, the question still remains as to whether evolutionary biology is enough to *justify* the absoluteness of the commandment to adhere to the ethic of knowledge or any other serious moral imperatives.

4. Even if natural selection is able to shed light on early and immature stages of moral development, this does not mean that it can fully explain each and every expression of morality. Evolutionary derivations of ethics generally ignore the fact that there can be qualitatively distinct stages in human moral development. The contemporary evolutionary naturalist's goal of accounting for our sense of duty ultimately as a mere matter of gene survival is suspect, therefore, because it fails to take into account the fact that there are various levels or stages of human moral development. After all, "morality" and "ethics" are terms that may refer to a wide range of dispositions and actions. As people move from childhood to adulthood, it is only gradually that they (sometimes) arrive at a habitually mature, self-sacrificing kind of moral existence. Can evolutionary biology be the foundational explanation of every instance of moral aspiration and activity?

In his *Descent of Man*, Darwin indicates that he is fully aware that moral improvement can be made both socially and individually. Ethical progress is possible, and the ruthlessness of natural selection—especially its disregard of the weak and powerless—should be reduced and even renounced in the social existence of genuinely moral human beings. However, many of Darwin's defenders today pay little attention to the stages through which moral development may pass. The typical Darwinian explanation of every level of ethical aspiration nowadays comes down to the same hypothesis: genes are trying to get into the next generation.

Following James Fowler and Michael Barnes, however, let us distinguish loosely three levels or stages in moral development: preconventional, conventional, and postconventional.[9] "Preconventional" morality is formed by a sense of rewards and punishments. Here the sense of obligation stems from fear of punishment and expectation of reward. It is rooted in a need for gratification and the instinct to avoid pain. This stage of moral life is characteristic of very young children and psychologically handicapped adolescents and adults. It is doubtful, however, that even mature people ever completely outgrow this stage. Perhaps evolutionary biology can shed some light on this level of moral existence.

Anticipating this book's next chapter, I want to add in passing that not only moral but also *religious* development has preconventional, conventional, and postconventional stages.[10] As long as people think of God as the source of regulations that one must follow to gain paradise and avoid hell, for example, they remain stuck in a relatively primitive, preconventional stage of religious development. I need to highlight this point because when evolutionary naturalists such as Dawkins and Dennett deal with what they call "God" or "religion," they usually have in mind a system of rewards and punishments characteristic of the most undeveloped stage of ethical and religious existence. They reject "theology" because they take it to be nothing more than a defense of the most childish kinds of moral and religious existence. What they fail to allow for is that there can be dramatic religious and moral growth (both personal and social) beyond the most immature versions, parallel to the growth of a child into an adult.

Moreover, atheistic evolutionists do not seem to notice that in the very act of condemning the childish religiosity and morality of most of their fellow humans, they too are appealing implicitly to timeless ethical ideals no less than theology does in its own justification of a more adult morality. Atheists also need an unassailable standard of "rightness" if they are to direct the rest of us authoritatively toward what they take to be a more mature sense of obligation. But what is it that makes their implicit moral ideals any "better" than those of the religiously and ethically immature? Unless they can point to *objective* criteria by which to make such a comparison or contrast, why should we pay any attention to them? If, as many evolutionary ethicists claim, *all* moral idealism is nothing more at bottom than a product of evolutionary adaptation and gene survival, then the atheistic evolutionist's sense of rightness is no more than an adaptation as well.

As I have already suggested, there is something self-subversive about any attempt to explain morality in evolutionary terms alone. However, just for the sake of argument, let us suppose that the ideas of adaptation, kin selection, gene survival, and other evolutionary factors (such as reciprocal altruism) can account for the earliest stages of moral development. Is evolutionary biology thereby justified in explaining the full developmental range of human moral action and aspiration by invoking the same set of biological factors in every case? Are there not mature, courageous, and heroic instances of human moral behavior that require a more robust explanation and justification than Darwinian biology can provide?

I shall address this question below. Before doing so, however, let us look at the second of our three (roughly drawn) stages of moral development: "conventional" morality. Here the sense of obligation stems not so much from fear of punishment or the need for gratification as from our longing to be accepted as part of a social group. The group to which we want to belong may be our family, schoolmates, gang, union, sorority, church community, military unit, political party, and suchlike. It is a natural instinct for members of many species to "belong," and this is especially true of human beings.

The conventional level of moral development may also seem, at least at first sight, to be purely adaptive. Conventional morality allows members of a species, including human beings, to exist in cooperative arrangements that enhance overall opportunities for successful gene replication. As the quotations from Darwin's *Descent of Man* at the beginning of this chapter show, Darwin himself was preoccupied mostly with what I am here calling the conventional stage of moral development. Regarded from a more contemporary biological perspective, conventional morality is just another means by which human genes can get into future generations.

It might seem once again, therefore, that evolutionary accounts of morality are enough. We may think of ourselves as highly "moral" simply because we have performed an altruistic act or made a sacrifice for the group's sake. But perhaps the same gene survival, kin selection, and reciprocal altruism that account for cooperativeness in other species also undergird our own sense of duty to one another within a group setting. Then there would be nothing especially supernatural or heroic about our ethical conduct, since the real agents of our altruistic activity are the packs of genes that we share with our kin. Here again, let us observe that religion can also become mixed up with conventional morality. Conventional morality is likely to look for religious sanctions to support its ethical precepts. The idea of "God" may therefore give a fictitious aura of eternal validity to a sense of duty that, to the evolutionist, is purely natural both in origin and function.

Nevertheless, even if conventional morality could be easily explained in evolutionary terms, there is a third, and much less commonplace, "postconventional" stage of moral development that defies any such reductionism. I am speaking of the kind of conduct shaped by the conviction that certain norms and actions are intrinsically "good" and that one is obliged to pursue them no matter what the cost to oneself, one's group, or the genes of one's relatives. There are exceptional human beings who have reached a level of moral development at which their actions, and indeed their entire lives, can be accounted for only on the assumption that they have been grasped by, and have responded to, an unconditional goodness.

At this third level of moral development, each of us is challenged to pursue timeless ideals placing demands on us that a purely naturalistic worldview cannot explain or justify. Evidence for this higher stage of moral existence can be found in the fact that even the evolutionary atheist has experienced and responded to such high ideals as that of being faithful to truth. The pursuit of truth for truth's sake could not become a serious ethical obligation if it were taken to be just one more way in which human genes are adapting and surviving. Hence, we may safely conclude that even the moral life of the evolutionary naturalist demonstrates that not every instance of morality can be explained or ultimately justified in evolutionary terms.

Ironically, we may find no better example of postconventional morality than in the way Charles Darwin lived his own life. This man's sterling character, his honesty, scientific integrity, generosity, and sensitivity to the suffering of others render him nearly unimpeachable, morally speaking, as almost everyone who knew him testified. Attempts to explain Darwin's own ethical uprightness as though it were mere adaptation rather than a response to timeless values seem almost blasphemous and do him no credit. Perhaps theology can be more respectful.

Theology and Evolutionary Naturalism

Without necessarily contradicting Darwinian *science*, Kant may very well have been right all along. If one adopts the "layered" approach to explanation that I have been advocating throughout this book, then an evolutionary narrative about how morality emerged and developed in the human sphere of life does not necessarily rule out a theological explanation: the highest moral idealism requires our having been touched at the deepest levels of our being by the presence and challenge of an infinite goodness. From the reading levels of science and natural history, our sense of duty appears to have an evolutionary origin and development; but at a deeper reading level, our moral aspiration may justifiably be interpreted as a *response* to the world's ultimate environment, the irresistibly attractive horizon of goodness that Christians and others call God.

Of course, evolutionary naturalists are ready with their predictable rebuttal to such a proposal. Morally heroic individuals, they will claim, are the human equivalents of the altruistic prairie dog. Saints and martyrs, especially if they are virgins or celibate, are programmed genetically to sacrifice their own reproductive opportunities so that the wider pool of human genes can more readily adapt and self-replicate. Exceptional moral conduct by certain human beings can still be naturalistically explained by such ideas as inclusive fitness. Genes are still driving the whole show.

However, there are two problems with a purely naturalist approach. First, there is still no unambiguous empirical evidence that gene survival is the ultimate explanation of human morality. But second—and more important—by trying to explain *every* instance of moral behavior in terms of adaptation, the gene-centered account of morality ends up explaining nothing. A naturalistic account, after all, has to account for *all* instances of moral obligation. If it fails to cover each and every expression of human obligation, it will not have fulfilled its own promise to be scientifically comprehensive. So, if any of the three levels of moral development we have just described does not lend itself to an exhaustively evolutionary account, then the sense of duty will remain a mystery, perhaps even open to theological understanding.

Darwin's *Descent of Man* left room for a theory of moral development, but most contemporary evolutionary naturalists make no allowances for the significant differences between a child's preconventional moral instincts, the conventional conduct of adolescents, and the moral idealism of adults such as Darwin. A biological understanding of morality cannot differentiate clearly between Martin Luther King's idealistic intransigence and a Nazi's sense that it is good to purify the race. Because of its incurable generality, a gene-survival account of morality ends up "explaining" mutually contradictory motivations and actions in terms of the very same sets of purely natural causes in every case. There is failure of logic here: if one kind of moral motivation or activity can be explained adequately by the interest that genes have in achieving immortality, then an opposing kind of moral motivation or activity cannot be adequately understood by appealing to exactly the same genetic influences.

It is not wrong to claim that human morality has at least something to do with the cooperation among members of a species and the kind of behavior that is indispensable to gene survival. If nobody among us were cooperative or altruistic, the human species would have perished long ago. For our species to last, genes obviously have to survive; and in the case of human beings, morality must have something to do with that outcome. But can gene survival be the *ultimate* cause of every moral aspiration as well as the adequate justification of the absolute and unconditional character of the demands that certain values (such as seeking truth, no matter what the cost) place on us?

The problem with evolutionary accounts of morality is that their generality prevents them from telling us anything significantly informative about our sense of duty. In that respect, they remind one of attempts to explain today's weather by saying that it is all caused by the laws of physics. This is not wrong, but it leaves out a lot. Whether the temperature is hot or cold outside today, the principles of thermodynamics are at work in the physical world, and so perhaps it is not wrong to say that heat exchanges explain the weather in both instances. If this were all that needed to be said, however, we would not need meteorologists; physicists would suffice.

Similarly, genetic transmission is going on whether people are being bad or good, cowardly or heroic. But something in addition to mere gene survival—or any other evolutionary causes—would have to account for the different levels and goals of moral life. Although evolutionary and other scientific accounts may be part of any richly layered understanding of morality, these cannot function coherently as *ultimate* explanation without subverting even the evolutionary naturalist's own sense of duty.

It is the business of theology, not of science, to look for ultimate explanations. So without having to reject or compete with evolutionary accounts of morality, theology may be brought into our discussion here as a distinct layer of explanation of morality. Allowing for the gradual evolutionary emergence of our moral responsiveness, theology may reasonably make the following claim: the absoluteness of certain moral demands (such as the imperative to seek truth, no matter what the cost) is justified if the *whole universe* out of which moral aspiration has emerged is itself pervasively grounded in an ultimate, transcendent goodness, in what the theistic faiths call God.

Theologically speaking, as I pointed out earlier, everything in nature participates in the inexhaustible depth dimension that classical theology and philosophy refer to as infinite being, truth, beauty, and goodness. This depth of inexhaustible goodness touches human minds and hearts in an especially intense way, even while it also stimulates the whole of nature to undergo the drama of evolutionary transformation. Our minds and hearts cannot grasp this elusive dimension of infinite goodness, but they can allow themselves to be grasped and transformed by it.

Morality, then, is both an outcome of natural evolutionary factors *and* a response to the divine. It is—at one and the same time—a product of physical or natural causes *and* of the universe's being drawn toward an infinite and never fully comprehended goodness. In this book's final chapter, I shall propose that the cosmic process and the drama of evolution are possible at all only because of the general responsiveness of the whole universe to a divine invitation to undergo the transformative drama of becoming *more*. Here I want only to suggest that our own moral striving is continuous with, and an extension of, the larger cosmic process and the drama of life as these respond to such a magnanimous invitation.

In our layered understanding of explanation, there is no inherent contradiction between a theological account of morality as a response to God on the one hand, and an evolutionary account of the gradual emergence of morality on the other. Contrary to evolutionary naturalism's totalistic claim of providing explanatory adequacy on the question of duty, theology and science may occupy logically distinct explanatory levels. They do not compete with each other but can jointly bring a richer intelligibility to the understanding of human morality than either can accomplish by itself.

Speaking theologically, human moral sensitivity, along with the whole restless universe out of which it has evolved, is *already* in the grasp of an infinite goodness. So the call of conscience is one with God's invitation to the whole of creation to enter into the transformative mystery of everlasting, self-sacrificing divine love. From the point of view of Christian theology, one must say that each morally inspired person is already quietly and lovingly embraced—without the slightest coercion—by this divine love. If this is true, then the unconditional character of moral obligation has an adequate explanation and justification that evolutionary biology cannot provide. At the same time, this theological layer of understanding is completely compatible with a scientific level of inquiry that seeks to uncover in more and more detail the evolutionary drama that has led to the emergence of our heightened sense of obligation.

Chapter 10

Devotion

Thus disbelief crept over me at a very slow rate, but was at last complete. The rate was so slow that I felt no distress, and have never since doubted even for a single second that my conclusion was correct. I can indeed hardly see how anyone ought to wish Christianity to be true; for if so the plain language of the text seems to show that the men who do not believe, and this would include my Father, Brother and almost all of my friends, will be everlastingly punished. And this is a damnable doctrine.
                              —*Charles Darwin,* Autobiography[1]

I am not sure whether it would not be wisest for scientific men quite to ignore the whole subject of religion.
                    —*Charles Darwin, in a letter to Joseph Hooker*[2]

If evolutionary biology can account for duty, maybe it can account for devotion as well. If Darwin's science provides the key to morality, perhaps it can also unlock the mystery of religion and worship. The term "devotion," one that Darwin used at times when speaking about religion, signifies not only the inclination to worship something sacred, but also the habit of surrendering one's whole being to *anything* that one takes to be absolutely important. In a broad sense, religion, as Paul Tillich has proposed, is "ultimate concern." Religion is our distinctively human tendency to enshrine something as unconditionally important to us, something without which our lives lack meaning, joy, and vitality. This "something" need not be the God of Western religions. It can also be something purely secular, such as the state or the stock market. It can also be science, single-minded devotion to which is known as scientism. Or it can be evolutionary theory itself. Evolutionary naturalism is a species of devotion that endows Darwinian science with the nearly infallible status of being the deepest available explanation of all animal and human behavioral traits, including religion.

Religion, in the sense of ultimate concern, has countless manifestations, both secular and sacred. In keeping with the theological focus of the present work, however, I am thinking here of the kind of religion that specializes in devotion to an unseen personal deity. To be more precise, I am concentrating here on belief in the God of biblical religion, the God of Abraham, Isaac, Jacob, the prophets, and Jesus. What light can Darwin's science shed on the inclination of so many people to worship the creative, redemptive, and responsive God of the Bible? Can Darwin's science *ultimately* account not only for morality and religion in general but also for the persistence of the idea of God?

Isn't it likely, evolutionary naturalists ask, that our theistic obsession is nothing more than an adaptation, a survival mechanism that helps our genes get into the next generation? Isn't belief in a personal God merely a product of guileful evolutionary processes that lead our brains to imagine that we are cared for by a benign providence? If so, belief in God is a grand illusion. Maybe this illusion helped our ignorant ancestors feel at home in an otherwise unbearable universe and in this way contributed to the human race's reproductive fitness. But after Darwin, isn't the idea of God finally exposed as pure fiction?

The *ultimate* reason why the idea of God persists today, at least according to many evolutionary naturalists, is because devotion to this illusion is still in some way biologically adaptive. Belief in a God who rewards and punishes causes people to work hard and take their lives seriously, regulating their activities, thoughts, and sexual behavior, guiding them and giving them hope as they bear and educate children, motivating them to cultivate life-enhancing virtues. In this cunning way, theistic belief promotes human gene survival. Thus, Darwin's science has now allowed enlightened people to understand what belief in God is really all about. It is one more way in which the human species' genetic endowment discovers a circuitous path to immortality. Our genes may not be the immediate cause of our tendency to believe in God, since cultural factors are also involved, but they are the ultimate explanation.[3]

Darwin himself never applied his ideas to theology in such an explicitly debunking manner. Even though he certainly thought of belief in God as adaptive, he never explicitly claimed that adaptation is all there is to it. However, many of Darwin's followers today are more daring, equipped as they are with an understanding of genes that Darwin did not have. By explaining theistic belief in terms of populations of genes striving to get themselves passed on to future generations, more than a handful of contemporary Darwinians are confident that they have explained the idea of God away for good. Hence, theology is now intellectually obsolete. To many evolutionary naturalists, the older and less scientific critiques of the God idea by the likes of Friedrich Nietzsche, Sigmund Freud, Karl Marx, and Jean-Paul Sartre are no longer worthy of much attention. Darwin's notion of natural selection combined with the more recent science of genetics provides a more empirically convincing explanation of why the idea of God came about at all and why it does not go away easily.

For a long time most evolutionists, like Darwin himself, were shy about trying to explain belief in God as a product of blind evolutionary selection and adaptation. But science has shown that so many other phenomena previously supposed to have nonnatural causes—like diseases and thunderstorms—can be accounted for in a purely natural way. So why not look at religion and theology naturalistically also? A good number of evolutionary scientists, psychologists, anthropologists, and philosophers now have as their goal the complete "naturalizing" of belief in God, along with all other kinds of religious expression. For an increasing number of scholars today, the power of Darwin's ideas to explain religion naturalistically is unparalleled. Biology after Darwin, they claim, is finally poised to give us the real reason for the persistence of theism without having to assume the actual existence of a self-revealing deity.

Darwinian Debunking

To support this thesis, the Darwinian debunkers, as I shall call them, start with several assumptions that seem undeniable to most evolutionists today. The first is that human behavior and cognitional tendencies are *inherited* no less than our anatomical and other physical characteristics are. The second is that inheritance—in the case of human beings, as in any other species—is a matter of populations of genes passing from one generation to the next. And the third hypothesis is that the human brain was optimized by evolution during the last few million years specifically to suit a hunter-and-gatherer type of existence. In that situation the hominid brain evolved various capacities essential for survival, such as skill in avoiding predators, and anatomically modern human beings eventually inherited essentially the same cerebral traits that earlier hunters and gatherers had acquired in their own survival strategies. This means that adaptive evolutionary pressures quite different from those operative today were the main sculptors of our brains. So it is no

wonder that human adaptation to contemporary historical and cultural circumstances is a formidable challenge, one not always successfully met.

But what does this evolutionary picture of human brain development have
to do with belief in God? To the evolutionary naturalist, religious belief of all
sorts must be adaptive, but how so? The anthropologist Pascal Boyer, in his
book *Religion Explained: The Evolutionary Origin of Species of Religious
Thought*, tells us how it all works.[4] The brain, Boyer admits, has no specifically religious instinct, but even now our brains possess tendencies that
earlier served the need for predator detection.[5] If our ancestors had not been
good at becoming aware of predators, they would have been eaten up, their
genes wouldn't have survived, and we wouldn't be here. But brains shaped
long ago by evolution to be on guard for unseen predators are ready-made
to look for hidden agencies of all kinds even today. The primeval habit of
preparing one's senses to encounter unseen predators, Boyer hypothesizes,
has fashioned human nervous systems and brains that even today can easily
conjure up imaginary supernatural beings also lying outside of the direct field
of vision. By heredity, human beings today still carry around brains that can
all too easily give rise to illusory belief in an unseen deity.[6]

So we are inclined to theistic devotion not because we have ever encoun-
tered God—since God does not exist—but simply because our ancestors
passed on to us genes with an adaptive propensity to manufacture illusions of
sacred unseen beings. These illusions helped our species adapt to an inherently hostile world for many thousands of years before science came along
to set us straight. Religion and theology kept our ancestors from looking too
far into what science, especially evolutionary biology, has now shown to be
the emptiness and indifference of the universe. By creating the fiction that
the universe is purposefully governed by a loving providence, belief in God
gave our prescientific predecessors a (fictitious) reason for living moral lives,
which in turn kept our species' genes from perishing.

So, according to Boyer's theory (one that Dawkins and Dennett also
endorse), with Darwin's help scientists can now understand naturalistically
why so many people persist in their longing for God. Although believers may
have thought that their faith was a response to the sacred presence of a self-
revealing God, Darwinian biology now shows that this faith is just an illusory
way of guaranteeing reproductive success.

And so it goes. The Darwinian debunkers of religion and theology follow
a long line of post-Enlightenment attempts to naturalize belief in God as
"nothing but" this or that. Sigmund Freud explained—or explained away—
the idea of God as a projection of infantile desires. Émile Durkheim treated
the idea of God as the illusory reflection of societal ideals. Karl Marx saw

religion and theology as a groundless superstructure erected over an economically unjust world. And Friedrich Nietzsche interpreted the Western obsession with God as a symptom of the all-too-human refusal to embrace life. According to our Darwinian debunkers, however, evolutionary biology has now given enlightened critics a much more scientific explanation of belief in God. It has decisively demystified centuries of spiritual hunger for God. Consequently, evolutionary naturalists now virtually ignore the older critiques of religion. Darwinian science has penetrated as deeply as one can go into explaining the annoying and obsolete addiction to belief in God, say the Darwinian debunkers.

Darwinian Leniency

Lovers of truth, therefore, should be willing to give up the idea of God as a "delusion" now that Darwinian science has shown it to be a product of adaptation and gene survival. We should all follow the example of Dawkins, Dennett, and other "new atheists" and let go of God as an anachronistic leftover from a preevolutionary age. However, other Darwinian debunkers are not always as hard on those of us who believe in God as are the new atheists and some of the earlier critics of religion. Nurtured by the Enlightenment, earlier demystifiers of theism such as Freud, Nietzsche, Bertrand Russell, Jean-Paul Sartre, W. K. Clifford, and Jacques Monod could not tolerate what they took to be the irrationality of belief. However, in contrast to that more severe and disciplined atheism, a neo-Darwinian perspective seems at times to foster a softer and more tolerant evaluation of religious illusions. Richard Dawkins's tirades against religion are an exception to such leniency, but this is because his atheism is more a product of the older rationalism than of evolutionary insight. Most other Darwinian critics of religion—and by "religion" I am referring at this point to a much wider set of devotional phenomena than just belief in God—are much gentler. This is because a gene-centered evolutionary approach has to admit that if our ancestors had not been religious, we would not be here.

In other words, if our Paleolithic and Neolithic predecessors had not cultivated the illusions of religion, they could never have covered up the harsh fact that the universe is essentially pointless. They needed the facade of faith to allow them to deny the tragic truth that the universe is indifferent to our fate. Religious faith helped scientifically illiterate generations look upon the universe as essentially benign, and this (false) impression allowed their genes to survive. Lucky for us, nature gifted our ancestors with an adaptive capacity for self-deception. Indeed, their inability to face the truth head-on—in the heroic way our Darwinian debunkers claim to do—is a gift for which we should be thankful! So nowadays, let's not be too hard on the still-deluded masses of people whose genes we share only because people of the past were capable of lying to themselves.

Embracing the antireligious creed of evolutionary naturalism, the Darwinian debunkers ironically have to be glad that our ancestors did not know the dark Darwinian truths that we do. So perhaps we should let people today continue to muddle along in their biologically fertile ignorance. A friend of mine, the philosopher Loyal Rue of Luther College, though he no longer believes in the personal God of Christianity, still promotes the persistence of religious illusions as indispensable to the long-term survival of our species. Following the Harvard evolutionist Edward O. Wilson, another Darwinian known to be quite easy on religious believers, Rue suggests that human survival thus far is in some measure due to our genetically based capacity for deceit. Throughout the evolution of mammalian life, the propensity for "guile" has been a saving "grace," including in human evolution. "The role of deception in human adaptive strategies," Rue writes, "has been so important that we may suspect it to be essential to our survival."[7] So there is no biologically compelling reason for humanity to give up its own adaptive religious lies now or in the future.[8]

According to Rue, religions are not least among the deceptive strategies that our genes manufacture to ensure their survival. Epistemologically speaking—as far as knowledge of truth is concerned—religions are objectionable, but the very unwillingness or inability of religious people to face the "truth" has the redeeming feature of being good for our genetic future. Enlightened Darwinians will have the savvy to see what is *really* going on in humanity's instinct for devotion, but they will not be in a big hurry to let everyone else know about it. A few learned people will realize that the masses of humanity have been tricked into an adaptive but fictitious supernaturalist trance by devious genes striving to live on, but they will not necessarily see any point in breaking the news to just anybody right away. In Rue's opinion, maybe we should deliberately foster the persistence of the vital "lie" of religious belief. Otherwise we may end up discarding one of our species' most effectively adaptive inventions, the capacity for creating religious illusions, without which our genes may become vulnerable to extinction.

Truth after Darwin

Loyal Rue is a kind and compassionate man, as I can testify personally, and it is out of genuine love for his fellow humans that he is moved to tolerate and even foster religion even though its truth value is questionable to him. From my personal conversations with him, however, he already knows that I have a different position on Darwin and the implications of evolution for religion. I agree that there is nothing inherently problematic about an evolutionary or even a gene's-eye perspective on religion and theology. Let us push such accounts as far as they can take us. Just as there is nothing wrong with looking at this page from the perspective of the chemistry of ink and paper, I have no objection to looking at religion scientifically through the lenses of evolutionary biology and genetics. Maybe we can learn something useful by telling the story of how brains prone to religious devotion began to take shape during the Pleistocene epoch.

However, none of this has anything whatsoever to tell us about the specific content of different creeds and diverse systems of religious understanding, or whether there is any truth to our own ideas about God. The Darwinian debunkers claim that evolutionary theory provides the ultimate explanation of why religion exists and that consequently theological explanation is no longer necessary or believable for the enlightened. But even the most refined scientific grasp of evolution cannot by itself tell us anything about the existence of God, or about the possible meaning of life and the larger cosmic drama.

Evolutionary constraints, as I have already said, are comparable to grammatical rules. Life has to adhere to them if it is to have continuity and coherence. However, learning these rules will not specify what the drama of life is really all about or where it is going, any more than your knowledge of syntax can tell you where my writing in this chapter or book is leading. I have to obey strict grammatical rules while writing this chapter, but learning what these rules are will by itself tell you nothing about what I have to say here or whether or not it is true. Likewise, a scientific mastery of the laws of physics, chemistry, and biology is not enough to determine whether life has a meaning, or the universe has a purpose, or whether God exists.

On the other hand, religions and theologies may, for all we know, have the capacity to pick up signals, however obscurely, of a dramatic profundity in life that science cannot reach. Unlike science, Christian theology, for example, prepares devotees to experience life on earth as an expression of God's creative spirit and power of renewal, as a foretaste and promise of final resurrection. And theology does not have to repudiate science to understand the life-process in this dramatic way. Scientific method, after all, is limited to seeking only physical explanations of everything. Science is certainly permitted to say something about religions, but science is a self-limiting method of understanding the natural world, not a worldview that stands in a competitive relationship with theology. Its modest method of analysis cannot provide a fundamental, ultimate, adequate, and exhaustively deep explanation of *anything* in the universe, let alone religion.

Evolutionary naturalists disagree. Jerry Coyne, as we saw earlier, wants to turn science into a worldview that can compete with theology for the single explanatory slot he considers to be available. Frederick Crews, a well-known American literary critic, likewise speaks for many intellectuals who have swallowed evolution in one big gulp as though it can provide a fundamental grasp of what life is all about. Darwin, Crews writes, provides "a more plausible framework than divine action for guessing how the human brain could have acquired consciousness and facilitated cultural productions, not excepting religion itself. It is this march toward successfully explaining the higher by the lower that renders Darwinian science a threat to theological dogma of all but the blandest kind."[9]

In accounting for religion and theology in this way, Crews, like other Darwinian naturalists I have mentioned, presents us with a forced option: one must choose evolutionary *rather than* theological explanations of religion or vice versa. However, this is like telling readers of the page in front of you to choose between its grammar and its content. Such an option makes no sense because grammar and content are distinct and noncompetitive layers of influence operative on this page. They are not rivals. And yet Crews's confusion of grammar with content is typical of the thought world of countless evolutionists who assume, without any evidential support, that evolution and theology are destined forever to contradict each other.

Crews considers all attempts to reconcile theology with evolution to be "evasions" of "truth." Science alone, he believes, can lead us to truth. His own devotional framework is an uncompromising scientism and evolutionary naturalism. In contrast to Loyal Rue's gentle tolerance of religious "lies," Crews is a throwback to the more hard-hitting modern critics of religion, who want people to grow up and, shedding the false comforts of religion, face the impersonal and indifferent world that Darwin has exposed to our view. This is why he is annoyed that today even some of the most renowned evolutionary naturalists are unwilling to impose such an onerous realism on the masses of people.

For example, Crews scolds the late paleontologist Stephen Jay Gould, who agreed with Dawkins and Dennett that Darwinism goes best with materialism but who became increasingly tolerant of religion not long before his death in 2002. Gould took to the idea that science and religious belief can get along well enough if they just stay in their respective corners. Let religion handle questions about meaning and values, and let science deal with the "facts," Gould proposed. He even claimed that he (an agnostic) and Pope John Paul II could agree on that much—even though the latter, I am certain, would never have accepted Gould's simplistic way of dividing the labor of science and religion.

According to Crews, in any case, Gould's overtures to the religious community amount to nothing less than a compromise with "truth." Even Gould, after all, had consistently held that all religious stories and theological ideas are nothing more than arbitrary expressions of the human need for values and meaning, not empirically warranted responses to God or divine revelation. Crews upbraids Gould and other indulgent Darwinians for failing to own up to the "true" implications of evolution and thus admit that the universe lacks any deep meaning or purpose since matter is really all there is. Crews prefers the Cornell evolutionist William B. Provine's blunt proclamation that in order to accept both Christian faith and Darwinian biology, "you have to check your brains at the church-house door."

In my own opinion, Crews is justified in pointing out Gould's logical laxity. It is entirely reasonable for Crews to insist that a materialist view of the world, to which Gould had consistently professed his allegiance, is incompatible with belief in God. Nevertheless, Crews can give no justification for his own declaration that scientific materialism is the ultimate truth underlying evolutionary biology. Scientific materialism is also a belief, one that has its origin in an even more fundamental devotion: scientism, the belief that science is the only reliable guide to truth. Crews is an unquestioning devotee of scientism and its recent offshoot, evolutionary materialism, in complete agreement with Dawkins and Dennett. He simply takes for granted that the "empirical attitude" of science is the sole reliable road to right knowledge and that ultimately reality is reducible to mindless matter. But this belief is itself incapable of empirical confirmation or scientific demonstration. Scientism, Crews fails to notice, is no less a matter of belief than is a theist's trust in God.

Scientism and evolutionary naturalism, I now emphasize, are themselves instances of what in this chapter I am calling devotion. Evolutionary naturalists put complete and often blind trust in Darwin's science to provide the kind of ultimate explanation that theology traditionally has professed to offer. So why shouldn't evolutionary naturalism be subjected to the same kind of Darwinian debunking that Darwinians extend toward other kinds of religious worship?

In other words, how can we be sure that an exclusivist and uncritical devotion to Darwinian accounts of life is any less a matter of evolutionary adaptation than adherence to the doctrines of other kinds of religious faith? Perhaps genes are tricking evolutionists into the naturalistic belief that Darwin's ideas are as deep as one can go in attempts to understand what life is really all about. If so, then by the very logic of evolutionary naturalism, one must also raise questions about its own claim to truth. Evolutionary naturalism once again shows itself to be a self-subverting worldview. In claiming that evolution can explain all of life—including religion and belief in God—evolutionary naturalists, far from telling us the truth, may themselves be merely adapting to the contemporary intellectual environment, one in which embracing a naturalistic brand of devotion is at times a necessary condition for academic survival.

Crews would surely reply that if we follow Darwin, there is no room left for a theological reading of life. But how does he know this to be the case? It is not within the capacity of science to say anything about the ultimate depths of being, and therefore whether theology is or is not trustworthy. Crews's decree springs from evolutionist devotionalism, not from science. Needless to say, devotional commitments are unavoidable. We all tend to enshrine some belief or belief system as fundamentally important and illuminating, and in this sense even the materialist is devout. But it seems prudent to ensure that our grounding beliefs are not self-contradictory, and evolutionary materialism fails to pass this test.

Why does it fail? Because evolutionary materialism is compelled by the logic of its own belief system to make cosmic mindlessness the ultimate foundation and explanation of the human mind. In doing so, it provides no good reason for a materialist such as Crews to trust his own mind, as in fact he does whenever he makes any of his confident claims, including his declaration that materialism is the real truth of Darwinian science. If mind is reducible to mindless matter in the final analysis—as it is for the materialist—and if human intelligence is a mere evolutionary adaptation to boot, why should anybody trust any of its claims?

Even Darwin occasionally wondered out loud why we should trust the mind if random variation and natural selection alone were able to account for it fully. "With me," he wrote to a friend, "the horrid doubt always arises whether the convictions of man's mind, which has been developed from the mind of the lower animals, are of any value or at all trustworthy. Would any one trust in the convictions of a monkey's mind, if there are any convictions in such a mind?"[10]

Crews stands with other Darwinian debunkers in trusting the complete adequacy of his own mind and of evolutionary biology to explain not only life and mind but also religion. Here, however, I do not wish to criticize his attraction to Darwinian science. Rather, I want only to question his devotion to evolutionary naturalism and the myth that Darwinian accounts can say anything about the truth or falsity of religious claims.

Furthermore, I suggest that the materialist worldview to which Crews is so devoted actually obscures the richness of the life-world as Darwin saw it. To grasp the real "truth" of evolution, Crews thinks we need to reduce all of life to the lifeless matter from which, according to his creed, all things come. His is a worldview in which life is ultimately resolvable into a blank deadness, a domain in which mindlessness lurks beneath everything. Imprisoned by these assumptions, Crews can have no appreciation of evolution as a drama in which something significant may still be working itself out. In his devotional system, the careful work of biologists, geologists, paleontologists, geneticists, embryologists, anatomists, and other scientists who have laid open the narrative of life—all this work becomes choked out in the cosmic lifelessness to which materialism eventually reduces everything.

Life and its evolution deserve a better devotional context. A more generous and liberating setting for evolution, I propose, is a biblical vision in which the world and life are framed by an ultimate environment of *promise*. The Bible gives us such a worldview, one in which ultimate reality—in other words, God—arrives from out of the future to give new life to the creation and fresh hope to human history. Here the fact of evolution finds its ultimate explanation in a universe opened by its creator to undreamed-of possibilities still hidden in the future. Always beyond reach, God abides in the depths of an elusive but forever-faithful future, which keeps opening the world to unpredictable outcomes. For these we must wait patiently and hopefully, with the expectation of being surprised. "Revelation," as theologian Wolfhart Pannenberg has put it, means "the arrival of the future," but we have to wait for it. God is the world's Absolute Future, as Karl Rahner speculates, but it transcends every image of the future that we ourselves can propose. We cannot grasp this future, Paul Tillich adds, but we can allow it to grasp us.[11] I recommend that we situate the drama of evolution in terms of such a vision of God and the future.

I freely admit that in this book's conversation with Darwin, I am looking at life from the perspective of Christian faith and hope. I cannot scientifically prove that evolution has its ultimate explanation in a God of promise and fidelity, nor is it appropriate even to try to do so. However, I am at least confident that there is no contradiction between a Christian theological setting and the discoveries of evolutionary science. What is more, I suggest that a world graced by the divine promise of an unpredictable and surprising future has the great advantage of not being reducible to the dead matter of the cosmic past, to which evolutionary materialism eventually leads. Evolution makes better sense if we locate it within a theological vision in which the cosmic past is liberated from lifelessness and mindlessness by God, the "power of the future."[12]

Theologically speaking, the promising God who opens up the world to a new future is the *ultimate* explanation of evolution. The future, not the dead past, is the foundation on which the world leans as it comes alive and undergoes its dramatic divinizing transformation. Let us now look more closely at this theological way of making sense of Darwin's discoveries.

Chapter 11

Deity

Who will at last give evolution its God?
—Pierre Teilhard de Chardin[1]

Christ is the end-point of the evolution, even the natural evolution, of all beings; and therefore evolution is holy.
—Pierre Teilhard de Chardin[2]

*C*harles Darwin, perhaps without intending to do so, has forced Christian theology to look at all aspects of life in a fresh way. These include design, diversity, descent, drama, depth, direction, death, duty, and devotion. Above all, however, Darwin invites theologians to reflect anew on what they mean by "deity." In the age of evolution, if we take science seriously, our thoughts about God cannot be exactly the same as before. To show why such revision is needed, in this final chapter I place Darwin in conversation with one of the most important Christian interpreters of evolution, the Jesuit priest and scientist Pierre Teilhard de Chardin (1881–1955). I doubt that any other Christian thinker has tried to make sense of evolution and belief in the God of Jesus Christ in such an innovative manner as has this modest French geologist.

After Darwin and the rise of modernity, we need a "new God," Teilhard states provocatively, but this does not mean that we need to sever all ties with traditional Christian teachings and creeds. Although his mind is fully open to evolutionary science, Teilhard's thoughts about God remain thoroughly rooted in the Bible and doctrinal tradition. But in the spirit of the Gospels he thinks we need to recapture, for our scientific age, Jesus' bold proclamation that something truly new and exciting is happening to the world right now. Evolution allows us to do so. Although Teilhard was not a professional theologian, his reflections on the meaning of God in the age of evolution are theologically sophisticated, and they merit special consideration here. In the contemporary conversation of theology with Darwin, Teilhard deserves to be taken more seriously than ever, and not just by Catholic theologians.

God up Ahead

Teilhard thinks about the God of evolution not as "up above" so much as "up ahead." God comes into the world from out of the future. Only by shifting to a futurist, hope-filled perspective can Christian thought connect the promises of God to Darwin's new picture of life. The universe, as evolution implies, is still coming into being. It is a work in progress, and for now it remains unfinished. It continues to be drawn toward an unpredictable and open future by the attractive power of a God who creates the world by offering it new possibilities for becoming *more*—opportunities for more intense and valuable modes of being. As a scientist, Teilhard accepts Darwinian evolution, though purged of any materialist overtones. But he is insistent that evolution has to do more with drama than design. For Teilhard, this drama, one in which the whole of creation undergoes a transformation from simple to more complex modes of being, carries a profound meaning that Christian faith can illuminate and that in turn can enliven Christian faith in our time.

The God of evolution continually creates a new world not *a retro*, by pushing things forward from the past, but *ab ante*, by drawing the world toward a new future from up ahead. The future is the primary dwelling place of God. Even though God is also present now and in the past, God is most powerfully effective *now* by opening the totality of things to an endlessly resourceful future. God is intimately involved in each present moment precisely by opening this moment to a new future. The world rests on this future, Teilhard says, as its "sole support." Whatever stability the universe has, in other words, lies not in the dispersed elements of its material past, but in the fidelity of the force that draws it toward the future. "The grandeur of the river is revealed not at its source but at its estuary."[3]

Here Teilhard's reflections remain close to the biblical understanding of God as the one who promises. He adds, however, that in the age of science we must now realize that God's promise is not just for Israel, the church, and human history, but also for the entire universe. The ultimate explanation of evolution is the coming (or advent) of God into the world from out of an endlessly expansive future. For Christians, the God who comes from the future becomes incarnate in Christ; in the ongoing evolution of life, the Spirit of Christ—the Holy Spirit—animates the whole of creation so that all things anticipate a final convergence in the wide embrace of God the Father. In the depths of evolution and cosmic process, what is *really* going on, therefore, is the Trinitarian drama: God the Father speaks the Word that becomes the incarnate center and goal of the universe, and the whole universe is now being transformed into God's bodily abode by the power of the Holy Spirit. As the apostle Paul expressed it centuries ago, all things are being brought to a head in Christ so that God may be "all in all" (1 Cor. 15:12–34).

Reading the drama of life in this way requires as its prelude a complex process of initiation into Christianity's creeds, rites, traditions, and theologies. Initiation into the world of scientific method and discovery alone will not lead you to see the life-process in the way I have just laid out. It is impossible to make your way directly from a scientific understanding of evolution to a Christian or any other religious way of understanding what is really going on in the depths of life. However, because of the deep *dramatic* connection between evolution and Christian faith, there is no contradiction between a scientific understanding of life in terms of natural selection on one level of understanding, and a theological reading of life as everlastingly meaningful on the other. One can in principle acquire expertise in both ways of looking at the life-process, and Teilhard is an excellent example of one whose vision has been immensely expanded by this stereoscopic deepening of the visual field. Only those who have lazily flattened out the world so that it fits into a materialistically hewed explanatory slot, or whose only criterion of theological rectitude is that of perfect design, only such people will ridicule the kind of expansiveness that rare figures such as Teilhard have made available to those with open minds and the capacity to hope.

As in the case of Whitehead, Teilhard's dramatic reading of life entails a dimension of permanence beneath the flux of cosmic events and in the depths of evolution. He locates this solidity not in the cosmic past, consisting of the multiple dispersed atomic and subatomic units on which scientific materialists base their understanding of nature, but on the horizon of the "up ahead," the future unity of all beings in God. Long before the twentieth-century arrival of the "theology of hope" (as represented by theologians such as Wolfhart Pannenberg and Jürgen Moltmann), Teilhard had already proposed that the God of evolution is one whose very essence is to be the world's future. His theology of evolution is an important part of the twentieth century's rediscovery of the future and the essentially eschatological substance of Christian faith.

Who Was Teilhard?

Teilhard was born into a large, religiously devout Catholic family in Auvergne, France, in 1881. He died in New York City on Easter Sunday, 1955. Ordained a Jesuit priest in 1911, he became a stretcher bearer during the First World War, where his bravery in battle eventually earned him entry into the Legion of Honor. Having already studied some geology as a seminarian and young priest, during the war he became increasingly convinced that evolutionary science now provides Christian theology with an appropriate framework for working out a new understanding of the biblical God of promise for our times. After the war he finished his doctoral studies in geology and was eventually dispatched to China, where he spent much of his scientific career.

Teilhard loved science and became a convinced evolutionist. He was one of the first scientists in the twentieth century to recognize that the whole universe is a still-unfolding drama, not simply a stage for the playing out of human history. However, he also realized that science by itself cannot tell us in depth what the cosmic drama and the evolutionary process are really all about. By looking back to the material simplicity of its causal past, analytical science dissolves the world into increasingly scattered bits of matter. In other words, the method of scientific analysis, if taken to its extreme, reduces nature to a primordial incoherence of particulate monads. For Teilhard, the world's coherence, and hence its intelligibility, resides not in its earliest stages of atomic dispersal but in a future state of ultimate unification. Theologically understood, it is ultimately by the power of God that the multiplicity of cosmic components is finally gathered into an intelligible unity. "To create," Teilhard often said, means "to unite," and it is ultimately God who brings unity to the multiple components of the cosmos. Right now, since the world is still coming into being, this ultimate unity, and hence the meaning of evolution, can be discerned only dimly, and only if we turn our attention in hope toward the world's climactic future in God:

> Like a river which, as you trace it back to its source, gradually diminishes till in the end it is lost altogether in the mud from which it springs, so existence becomes attenuated and finally vanishes away when we try to divide it up more and more minutely in space or—what comes to the same— to drive it further and further back in time. The grandeur of the river is revealed not at its source but at its estuary.[4]

Here Teilhard is seeking a distinctively post-Darwinian understanding of God. Theologically, he is completely comfortable with Darwin's revolution and indeed enthusiastic about it. Whether Darwin himself would have warmed to Teilhard's religious embrace of evolution is impossible to say. We need to recall, however, that the God that Darwin eventually disowned was the severely limited designer deity of William Paley and nineteenth-century natural theology, not the biblical God, which some contemporary theologians rightly refer to as the "power of the future."[5] Teilhard would have wanted nothing to do with Darwin's God either. Instead, he was most impressed by the remarkable consonance between evolution and a biblically based, fully incarnational, and eschatological sense of the God who is coming. The general framework of his theology of evolution is a hope-filled Christian faith, especially as expressed in the letters of the apostle Paul.

Teilhard's main work is *The Phenomenon of Man*, published only after his death in 1955.[6] His Christian vision of evolution began to take shape during World War I, and it was while working as a geologist in China between the wars and during World War II that he found time to elaborate on it extensively in the *Phenomenon*. However, he failed to gain permission from his church to publish the *Phenomenon* and many other writings on faith and evolution while he was alive. A defensive reaction to Darwin was still prevalent in official Catholicism during the first half of the twentieth century, and Teilhard's ideas on evolution and Christianity seemed too adventurous to his ecclesiastical censors. Church officials were especially concerned that an evolutionary understanding of human emergence would undermine Christian teachings about original sin. Today the shadow of suspicion under which some Catholic ecclesiastics formerly held Teilhard has virtually disappeared except among the most reactionary devotees of pre–Vatican II spirituality. Documents promulgated by the Second Vatican Council clearly bear the stamp of the Jesuit geologist's evolutionary theology.

In my opinion, therefore, even today there is no better place for Christian theology to initiate a conversation with Darwin about God than by looking at Teilhard's synthesis of evolution and faith. Here what stands out are, first, Teilhard's refusal to protect Christian thought from a close encounter with evolutionary science; and second, his sense of the need to expand and deepen our understanding of God in keeping with science's discovery of the drama of life and the ongoing enlargement of astronomy's picture of the cosmos, an impression that has grown by leaps and bounds since Darwin's day.

Timid theological minds still consider Teilhard's magnification of the universe and his corresponding enlargement of the concept of God as nearly heretical, but Teilhard is no more innovative and controversial than many other Christian thinkers have been in their own times. For example, Justin, Origen, Irenaeus of Lyons, Gregory of Nyssa, Augustine of Hippo, Thomas

Aquinas, Martin Luther, John Calvin, Friedrich Schleiermacher, and Paul Tillich—all have been quite adventurous in their own attempts to make sense of Christianity in their own specific cultural and historical settings. For Teilhard, the intellectual context for any believable theology today is shaped primarily by science, and especially its new story of an unfinished universe. So what is needed theologically is a thoroughgoing reinterpretation of Christian teaching about God, Christ, creation, incarnation, redemption, and eschatology in keeping with Darwin's unveiling of life's long evolution and contemporary cosmology's disclosure of the ongoing expansion of the heavens.

The first step toward the needed theological revision, however, is to distinguish evolutionary science from the philosophical materialism that has cramped the thought world of so many scientific thinkers since long before Teilhard's time and that persists today. Teilhard is convinced that evolution is not reducible to a reshuffling of atoms over time, and he would have rejected Dawkins's claim that at its deepest level evolution is a river of genes flowing from one generation blindly to the next. Although he accepts the fact that atoms are being reshuffled and genes are flowing in evolution, he is convinced that something much more meaningful is also occurring in evolution's dramatic depths, something that those who have been initiated only into the world of scientific naturalism will simply not be able to see.

The prevalent materialism among evolutionists since the time of Darwin declares that nothing deeper than the surface commotion of mindless material activity is taking place as the universe moves from its early elemental multiplicity to the recent emergence of minds and morality. However, as Teilhard insists, one would have to be deliberately blind and almost willfully unempirical to view evolution as no more than this. A wider (dramatic) vision allows one to see that in evolution the universe has always aimed to become *more*. It has never ceased being restless for increasing complexity, consciousness, freedom, and intense beauty. The evidence is all around us. Indeed, our own existence and remarkable capacity for thought, freedom, creativity, and goodness is information enough that the universe has become *more* over the course of time.

Evolutionary materialism, however, is mostly blind to the newly emergent sphere of *thought* that has come so recently into the universe, at least on earth. Why, Teilhard asks, should open-minded empirical observers leave human subjectivity and the astonishing world of thought out of a full picture of nature, especially when trying to understand what evolution is all about? Evolutionary materialists, by trying to reduce life and mind to lifeless and mindless elemental physical components, miss out on so much of what is really going on in nature. Teilhard is convinced that if we but open our eyes, we can *see* much more going on in evolution than the narrow filter of materialism allows to get through. Evolutionary science makes the most sense if we place it in a nonmaterialist metaphysical setting, one that gives priority to the future rather than the past.

When interpreted materialistically, evolution becomes less intelligible, not more intelligible. Trying to explain life by reducing it, as materialists do, to the earlier-and-simpler physical elements and processes lying in the dead past is a sure way to lose contact with the evolutionary drama in which "more being" gradually comes onto the cosmic scene, at least over the long haul.

Teilhard seeks, therefore, to replace the materialist "metaphysics of the past" with what might be called a "metaphysics of the future," a worldview in which what is "really real" comes into the field of our vision only as we look toward the final unification of the scattered cosmic elements in God. This futurist understanding of creation has been all but lost during the long centuries of Platonically shaped theology, which pictures God as an eternal presence, as unchanging Being, vertically and hierarchically above and outside of the world of becoming. After Darwin, however, the created world seems more at home in a biblical setting, one attuned to the Abrahamic and early Christian intuition that ultimate reality comes into the present as an ever-renewing future.

Teilhard's Layered Understanding of Life

During his lifetime, Teilhard had gained the highest esteem of his fellow scientists and was recognized as one of Asia's top geologists, so there can be no question about his scientific credentials. However, in the *Phenomenon* he was also doing more than science usually does, and some readers have found the book's literary genre confusing. He was reading life dramatically at one level and scientifically at another, both in the same book. This helps to explain why his best-known book has not always met with approval by evolutionary scientists. Teilhard, who clearly knew how to distinguish science from theology, unfortunately assumed that his readers would be able to differentiate the two levels at which he was reading the life-story. This was too generous an assumption on his part, since many who have tried to read the *Phenomenon* have been unprepared to look at evolution in both scientific terms and its dramatic depths simultaneously. Ian Barbour, an expert in the field of science and religion, rightly suggests therefore that readers should approach the *Phenomenon* not as a strictly scientific treatise but as a contribution to the theology of nature.[7]

Many critics of Teilhard have missed this point. For example, the Nobel-Prize-winning biochemist Jacques Monod, a self-described materialist, reproached Teilhard for looking for a deeper purpose in evolution than science can discern.[8] Stephen Jay Gould was so irked by Teilhard's conviction that there is a meaningful direction to evolution that he tried to deface Teilhard's reputation completely by tying him, without the slightest bit of incriminating evidence, to the infamous Piltdown Man hoax.[9] Daniel Dennett calls Teilhard a "loser" for rejecting the materialist worldview that he and Dawkins are unable to distinguish from evolutionary science.[10] With only a few exceptions, British scientists and theologians still ignore Teilhard because of one misleading and intemperate book review of the *Phenomenon* written by the eminent scientist Peter Medawar in *Mind* magazine soon after the book was translated.[11] In general, Teilhard's work has been misunderstood and increasingly ignored by scientists and Christian theologians alike.

This is unfortunate as far as any significant theological conversation with Darwin is concerned. I believe any such exchange today cannot profitably avoid making Teilhard a major part of the conversation. In doing so, it will certainly be necessary to bring Teilhard's science up to date, especially on the role of genes in evolution; this should not be hard to do. And second, it will be essential to distinguish carefully between Teilhard the scientist and Teilhard the theologian. Teilhard, as I said earlier, knew the difference between evolutionary science and his theological interpretation of it; but in some of his writings, he did not always make this distinction explicit enough for his readers.

To interpret evolution in a Christian manner, Teilhard had to challenge the materialist ideology that prevents most evolutionists from seeing through to the dramatic depths of the life-story. What then did he "see" beneath the materialist misreading of evolution? In the first place—and this is visible to anyone—on our own planet he saw that natural processes have successively brought about the realm of matter (the *geosphere*), then life (the *biosphere*), and most recently the sphere of mind, the *noosphere*. The noosphere is the world of "thought" made possible not only by the emergence of individual human minds but also by the increasingly elaborate global communications networks, educational institutions, cultural creativity, science, politics, economics, and technological achievements.

Why, Teilhard wondered, do most evolutionary naturalists fail to see that the noosphere, the planet-encompassing phenomenon of thought, is part of the world's evolution, and not just an arbitrary human addendum having little or nothing to do with the universe's own essence and meaning? On earth, the flowering of the noosphere over the last several thousand years is an extension of evolution and cosmic history, so it should be of interest to biology and

cosmology, and not just to the social sciences. Geologists, too, should recognize the noosphere as a new emergent layer now being deposited over the
lower levels of the fossil record, continuous with the layered way in which
earth's history evolves. Unfortunately, however, the emergent phenomenon
of thought remains off the map of the world as most evolutionary naturalists
picture it.[12] As a result of this omission, evolutionary naturalism still offers
only a diminished picture of what is *really* going on in the drama of life.

As far as Teilhard's theological vision is concerned, on the other hand, it
means a great deal that the world of thinking persons and the phenomenon
of thought are part of nature's evolution rather than something only inci-
dental to it. The domain of thought has its proper home in nature, and this
places in doubt the evolutionary materialist's assumption that the universe
is essentially mindless and hence devoid of purpose. Seeing that the recent
emergence of thought in evolution is connected seamlessly to the whole of
cosmic history, Teilhard insists that a purely mindless realm of matter has
never actually existed. Matter has always been pregnant with life, mind, and
"spirit" from the time of cosmic origins.

As long as the universe is thought of in a strictly materialist manner, it will
appear to be impermeable to divine influence. But the character of the universe is such that it has never been utterly mindless and spiritless at any time.
So at least in Christian terms, it is always open to the creative movement of
the Holy Spirit. Materialism has no place for either "thought" or the influence
of God in nature. Yet it should be clear by now that our own consciousness
and the noosphere are part of nature, and that "thought" has been latent in
matter from the outset. This means that there never could have been any
period in natural history when the universe was closed off to the influence of
God's unifying, creative Spirit.

Divine action in the world may be hard to understand as long as nature is
taken to be essentially mindless, but it turns out that the very idea of mindless
(or spiritless) matter is a logical illusion, stemming from science's inability
to "see" the interior side of matter that comes out into the light of day most
explicitly in the evolution of human consciousness and the noosphere. It is
the interior vein of "consciousness" running throughout cosmic history, and
especially in the dramatic depths of life, that allows the Spirit of God to
penetrate the natural world, luring it toward more intense modes of being.[13]
This interior side of nature, a strain invisible to science, also allows for the
incarnate and now-risen Christ to gather the entire universe, physically and
not just metaphorically, into his eucharistic body.[14]

Our own interiority, including our reflective self-awareness, is just as
much part of the natural world as plants, mountains, and oceans; but most

evolutionary naturalists ignore this subjective aspect, even their own sub-jectivity, as though it were not part of nature. In human beings the self-transforming universe has now become luminously conscious of itself; but by their metaphysics of the past, materialists are forced to reduce everything to unconsciousness, including their own minds. Then they try to "explain" the puzzling emergence of human minds as an evolutionary fluke that just happened to pop into existence accidentally out of an essentially mindless and impersonal universe. To Teilhard, this impoverished outlook buries the whole "point" of evolution beneath the rubble of incoherence. The material-ist project of explaining mind in terms of mindless stuff makes the very exis-tence of mind inexplicable even while, ironically, the materialist is relying on his or her mind to explain it.

A Post-Darwinian Spirituality

Christianity, Teilhard is convinced, provides a coherent alternative to mate-rialism's reading of evolution. The wellspring of evolution is the incarnation of God in Christ. The God who is coming and who takes flesh in Jesus is the foundation on which the universe leans "as its sole support." What is *really* going on in evolution, therefore, is that God is becoming increasingly incar-nate in the world, and the world is "exploding upward into God."[15] Beneath the surface of nature, about which science speaks analytically and reduc-tively, what is going on is the eternal drama of God's creativity, descent into the world, and promise of final renewal.

Nothing in this drama runs contrary to science. It's just that the drama goes on at a level lying too deep for science to grasp. Furthermore, by itself alone science cannot see that the world is still open to becoming even *more* as it moves further toward the future. However, in tune with the apostle Paul's theology, an evolutionary theology suggests that the body of Christ, which in a real sense includes the whole cosmos, is still in the process of being formed. Each of us has something to contribute to the world's ongoing creation and the building up of Christ's body—especially through acts that bring unity and overcome division. Every eucharistic celebration is a declaration of "what is really going on" in the universe even now: the risen Christ continues to trans-form the whole world, gathering us, our labor and achievements, our joys and sufferings, along with the entirety of life's long struggle and the whole cosmic process—gathering it all into the formation of his own body.[16]

It is lamentable to Teilhard that so many Christians go through life assum-ing that their existence has little or nothing to do with the ongoing creation of the universe. Too often we have thought that Christ's salvific role is that of liberating our souls *from* the universe rather than making us part of the great work of renewing and extending God's creation. But the Darwinian revolution invites theology to understand that each of us is commissioned to be part of the cosmic and living drama in which *the universe* still has room for transfiguration into something *more*.

Evolutionary science invites theology to entertain the thought that a transformative drama had already been going on in the universe long before human beings arrived on the scene. That we have the backing of a universe-in-the-making can give substance to our hopes, and energy to our moral aspirations. Evolution helps Christian theology read the evangelical proclamation of a new creation with a spirit of adventure that it might not otherwise have. This is why a theological encounter with Darwin is so important for the renewal of Christianity today.

Unfortunately, contemporary spirituality, theology, and ethical reflection have generally failed to take into account the fact of evolution and the cosmic drama. Lacking a sense that our own lives are part of a cosmic stream that flows, however haltingly at times, toward more intense modes of being, we expel from our spiritual and moral lives an enlivening stimulus to creative action. Even while trying to be virtuous, we end up drifting aimlessly in what seems to be no more than a vale of tears, in which we limit our lifework to purifying ourselves of contamination by the world.

In his "Mass on the World," Teilhard proposes an alternative way to understand the worthwhileness of our lives after Darwin.[17] We are not here just to spin our moral wheels while we wait to be rescued by God's decisive deliverance. What we should be awaiting and fostering is a *cosmic* transfiguration, not just a transfer of human souls to another world. The distinctively human virtues of faith, hope, and love are rooted not only in the human heart but, deeper yet, in a *universe* that has always been feeling its way forward toward fulfillment in God. Our practice of virtue should not be felt as a break with the cosmos but as essential to its ongoing creation.

Since many sensitive people these days are seeking a steady foundation for a global and ecologically responsible ethic, Teilhard's wide cosmic perspective deserves careful attention all the more. Up until now, unfortunately, awareness of the dramatic character of the universe and life has been absent from most attempts to forge a planetary moral consensus. Most professional ethical reflection is still excessively anthropocentric, blind to the fact that the earth and our humanity are folded into an immense universe, in which a mysterious "working out" has been under way for billions of years before our own recent arrival. Darwin's science allows Christians to realize that our lives can be ennobled, and our ethical action animated, by knowing that we and the earth have an important part to play in the much-larger cosmic and Christic drama of creation.

Most traditional, modern, and contemporary spiritualities have failed to connect human life to what is going on in the universe. Steeped in evolution, Teilhard instructs us that the human phenomenon, with its spiritual and moral aspirations, is a "function of sidereal evolution of the globe, which is itself a function of total cosmic evolution."[18] Overlooking the cosmic and evolutionary context of our lives amounts to cutting ourselves off from the very roots of vitality. Darwin's science, however, allows us now to tie our search for the kingdom of God and our building up of the body of Christ into the larger cosmic drama of creation. Adopting a cosmic, evolutionary spirituality does not mean that we would be permitted to stop performing the small and tedious tasks of everyday life. But an evolutionary perspective lets us appreciate that even the most mundane duties contribute to the noble enterprise of bringing a whole universe closer to unity and fulfillment in God.

Evolution allows us to realize that human beings are invited to participate in the great work of creation. If we fail to keep this evolutionary perspective alive, our sense of ethical obligation—and for the Christian, the following of Christ—is in danger of being reduced to blind obedience to arbitrary imperatives and divine commands, or perhaps simply to seeking a reward in the hereafter. In that case, ethical life becomes, in Teilhard's words, a matter of "killing time," and redemption becomes a matter of "harvesting souls" from a pointless universe. After Darwin, Christian theology can do better than this. Even though Darwin himself seemed oblivious to the potential his discoveries have to stimulate theological, spiritual, and ethical renewal, his theory of evolution is a great gift to Christian theology and spirituality as they seek to interpret Jesus' revolutionary understanding of God for our own age and future generations.

Notes

INTRODUCTION

1. Introduction to Darwin's *On the Origin of Species*, 6th ed. (New York: Collier Books, 1962), 5.

2. Daniel C. Dennett, *Darwin's Dangerous Idea: Evolution and the Meaning of Life* (New York: Simon & Schuster, 1995), 63.

3. Theodosius Dobzhansky, "Nothing in Biology Makes Sense Except in the Light of Evolution." *American Biology Teacher*, 35 (1973): 125–29.

4. See Richard Dawkins, *The Blind Watchmaker* (New York: W. W. Norton & Co., 1986); idem, *River out of Eden* (New York: Basic Books,1995); idem, *Climbing Mount Improbable* (New York: W. W. Norton & Co, 1996); idem, *The God Delusion* (New York: Houghton Mifflin, 2006); and Dennett, *Darwin's Dangerous Idea*; idem, *Breaking the Spell: Religion as a Natural Phenomenon* (New York: Viking, 2006).

CHAPTER 1: DARWIN

1. For citations of Darwin used in this book, readers may easily consult *The Complete Works of Charles Darwin*, http://darwin-online.org.uk/. My citations of Darwin's most famous book are from the sixth edition of *The Origin of Species* (1872; repr., New York: Random House, 1993), http://darwin-online.org.uk/content/frameset?viewtype=side&itemID=F391&pageseq=1.

2. See http://www.darwinproject.ac.uk/content/view/152/144/.

3. See http://www.darwin-literature.com/The_Autobiography_of_Charles_Darwin/1.html.

4. See http://www.darwinproject.ac.uk/darwinletters/calendar/entry-3154.html.

CHAPTER 2: DESIGN

1. Darwin, *Origin of Species,* 612, http://www.darwinproject.ac.uk/darwinletters/calendar/entry-2501.html.

2. See http://darwin-online.org.uk/content/frameset?itemID=F1497&viewtype=text&pageseq=1.

3. Janet Browne, *Charles Darwin: The Power of Place* (Princeton, NJ: Princeton University Press, 2003), 6.

4. Jerry A. Coyne, *Why Evolution Is True* (New York: Viking, 2009).

5. See http://www.tnr.com/story_print.html?id=1e3851a3-bdf7-438a-ac2a-a5e381a70472.

6. See http://whyevolutionistrue.wordpress.com/2009/04/22/truckling-to-the-faithful-a-spoonful-of-jesus-helps-darwin-go-down/.

7. Coyne, *Why Evolution Is True*, 122.

8. Ibid.

CHAPTER 3: DIVERSITY

1. Darwin, *Origin of Species*, 360.

2. Ibid., 260.

3. Ibid., 112.

4. Philip Kitcher, *Living with Darwin: Evolution, Design, and the Future of Faith* (New York: Oxford University Press, 2009), 124.

5. See Christopher Mooney, SJ, *Theology and Scientific Knowledge* (Notre Dame, IN: University of Notre Dame Press, 1996), 162.

6. Paul Tillich, *The New Being* (New York: Charles Scribner's Sons, 1955), 48.

CHAPTER 4: DESCENT

1. Darwin, *Origin of Species*, 261.

2. Cited by Browne, *Charles Darwin*, 68.

3. See http://www.darwinproject.ac.uk/darwinletters/calendar/entry-2534.html.

4. Cited by William P. Phipps, *Darwin's Religious Odyssey* (Harrisburg, PA: Trinity Press International, 2002), 89.

5. Here I am adapting ideas of Michael Polanyi, "Life's Irreducible Structure," in *Knowing and Being*, ed. Marjorie Grene, 225–39 (London: Routledge & Kegan Paul, 1969).

6. The expression "Absolute Future" is that of theologian Karl Rahner in *Theological Investigations*, vol. 6, trans. Karl and Boniface Kruger (Baltimore: Helicon, 1969), 59–68.

7. See Ted Peters, *God—the World's Future: Systematic Theology for a New Era*, 2nd ed. (Minneapolis: Fortress Press, 2000).

CHAPTER 5: DRAMA

1. Browne, *Charles Darwin*, 66–67.

2. Michael Polanyi, *Personal Knowledge: Towards a Post-Critical Philosophy* (New York and Evanston: Harper & Row, Harper Torchbooks, 1958).

3. Hans Jonas, *Mortality and Morality* (Evanston, IL: Northwestern University Press, 1996), 60, 165–97.

4. Chet Raymo, "Intelligent Design Happens Naturally," *Boston Globe*, May 14, 2002.

5. David Barash, "Does God Have Back Problems Too?" *Los Angeles Times*, June 27, 2005.

6. See Holmes Rolston III, *Science and Religion* (New York: Random House, 1987), 144–46.

7. John Henry Newman, *The Idea of a University* (Garden City, NY: Image Books, 1959), 411.

CHAPTER 6: DIRECTION

1. See http://darwin-online.org.uk/content/frameset?viewtype=text&itemID=F373&keywords=in+life+view+grandeur+of+this+is+there&pageseq=508.

2. Pierre Teilhard de Chardin, *Hymn of the Universe*, trans. Gerald Vann (New York: Harper Colophon, 1969), 119.

3. Alfred North Whitehead, *Adventures of Ideas* (New York: The Free Press, 1967), 265.

4. Stephen Jay Gould, *Ever since Darwin* (New York: Norton, 1977), 12–13.

5. Simon Conway Morris, *Life's Solution: Inevitable Humans in a Lonely Universe* (New York: Cambridge University Press, 2003).

6. S. E. Luria, *Life: The Unfinished Experiment* (New York: Charles Scribner's Sons, 1973), 148.

7. George Gaylord Simpson, *The Meaning of Evolution*, rev. ed. (New York: Bantam Books, 1971), 314–15.

8. Richard Dawkins, *River out of Eden*, 96.

9. Henri Bergson, *Creative Evolution*, trans. Arthur Mitchell (Lanham, MD: University Press of America, 1983).

10. Whitehead, *Adventures of Ideas*, 265.

11. Alfred North Whitehead, *Process and Reality*, ed. David Ray Griffin and Donald W. Sherburne, corrected ed. (New York: The Free Press, 1978), 105.

12. See John B. Cobb Jr. and David Ray Griffin, *Process Theology: An Introductory Exposition* (Philadelphia: Westminster Press, 1976); Whitehead, *Adventures of Ideas*, 252–96.

13. Whitehead, *Process and Reality*, 111. See also Cobb and Griffin, *Process Theology*.

CHAPTER 7: DEPTH

1. Robert Pippin, ed., *Nietzsche: Thus Spoke Zarathustra*, trans. Adrian Del Caro (Cambridge: Cambridge University Press, 2006), 264.

2. Gerard Manley Hopkins, "God's Grandeur," http://www.bartelby.com/122/7.html.

3. See Huston Smith, *Forgotten Truth: The Primordial Tradition* (New York: Harper & Row, 1976), 97.

4. Paul Tillich, *The Shaking of the Foundations* (New York: Charles Scribner's Sons, 1948), 56.

5. Ibid., 57.

6. Dennett, *Darwin's Dangerous Idea*, esp. 61–84.

CHAPTER 8: DEATH

1. See http://www.darwinproject.ac.uk/darwinletters/calendar/entry-5307.html.

2. Pierre Teilhard de Chardin, *How I Believe*, trans. René Hague (New York: Harper & Row, 1969), 43–44.

3. Whitehead, *Process and Reality*, 340.

4. Paul Tillich, *The Eternal Now* (New York: Charles Scribner's Sons, 1963), 33–34.

5. Ibid.

6. Alfred North Whitehead, *Science and the Modern World* (New York: The Free Press, 1925), 191–92.

7. Charles Hartshorne, *The Logic of Perfection* (LaSalle, IL: Open Court Publishing Co., 1962), 250.

8. Whitehead, *Process and Reality*, 346.

9. Tillich, *The Eternal Now*, 35.

10. Whitehead, *Process and Reality*, 345–51.

11. Ibid., 346.

12. Ibid.

13. See Whitehead, *Adventures of Ideas*, 62, 183–85, 265.

14. This is an insight that Teilhard de Chardin expresses in many of his works without developing it at length theologically.

CHAPTER 9: DUTY

1. See 1:73, http://darwin-online.org.uk/content/frameset?itemID=F937.1&viewtype=text&pageseq=1.

2. Comment to Frances Power Cobb, cited by Browne, *Charles Darwin*, 297.

3. See Robert Wright, *The Moral Animal: Evolutionary Psychology and Everyday Life* (New York: Pantheon Books, 1994).

4. Matt Ridley, *The Origins of Virtue: Human Instincts and the Evolution of Cooperation* (New York: Penguin Books, 1998), 12.

5. See Jerome H. Barkow, Leda Cosmides, and John Tooby, eds., *The Adapted Mind: Evolutionary Psychology and the Generation of Culture* (New York: Oxford University Press, 1992).

6. Jacques Monod, *Chance and Necessity*, trans. Austryn Wainhouse (New York: Vintage Books, 1972), 175–80.

7. Ibid.

8. As made famous by William James's important essay "The Will to Believe," in *The Will to Believe, and Other Essays in Popular Philosophy* (New York: Longmans, Green, & Co., 1931).

9. James W. Fowler, *Stages of Faith: The Psychology of Human Development and the Quest for Meaning* (San Francisco: Harper & Row, 1981); and Michael Barnes, *Stages of Thought: The Co-evolution of Religious Thought and Science* (New York: Oxford University Press, 2000).

10. See Fowler, *Stages of Faith*; and Barnes, *Stages of Thought*.

CHAPTER 10: DEVOTION

1. Nora Barlow, ed., *The Autobiography of Charles Darwin* (New York: Norton, 1958), 86.

2. Cited by John Hedley Brooke, "Charles Darwin on Religion" (2008), http://www.issr.org.uk/darwin-religion.asp.

3. Robert Hinde, *Why Gods Persist: A Scientific Approach to Religions* (New York: Routledge, 1999); Walter Burkert, *Creation of the Sacred: Tracks of Biology in Early Religions* (Cambridge, MA: Harvard University Press, 1996); Pascal Boyer, *Religion Explained: The Evolutionary Origins of Religious Thought* (New York: Basic Books, 2001); Scott Atran, *In Gods We Trust: The Evolutionary Landscape of Religion* (New York: Oxford University Press, 2002); David Sloan Wilson in *Darwin's Cathedral: Evolution, Religion, and the Nature of Society* (Chicago: University of Chicago Press, 2002) argues that religion is adaptive at the group level as well as at the levels of the individual and the gene.

4. Boyer, *Religion Explained*, 137–67.

5. Ibid., 145.

6. Ibid., 137–67.

7. Loyal Rue, *By the Grace of Guile: The Role of Deception in Natural History and Human Affairs* (New York: Oxford University Press, 1994), 125–26.

8. Ibid., 82–127.

9. Frederick Crews, "Saving Us from Darwin," *New York Review of Books*, part 1, October 4, 2001; part 2, October 18, 2001.

10. Charles Darwin, letter to W. Graham, July 3, 1881, in *The Life and Letters of Charles Darwin*, ed. Francis Darwin (New York: Basic Books, 1959), 285.

11. Wolfhart Pannenberg, *Faith and Reality*, trans. John Maxwell (Philadelphia: Westminster Press, 1977), 58–59; see Jürgen Moltmann, *The Experiment Hope*, ed. and trans. M. Douglas Meeks (Philadelphia: Fortress Press, 1975), 48; Rahner, *Theological Investigations*, 6:59–68; Paul Tillich, *Shaking*, 27; Peters, *God—the World's Future*. I have developed this theme at more length in my book *The Promise of Nature: Ecology and Cosmic Purpose* (Mahwah, NJ: Paulist Press, 1993).

12. See Pannenberg, *Faith and Reality*; and Wolfhart Pannenberg, *Toward a Theology of Nature*, ed. Ted Peters (Louisville, KY: Westminster/John Knox Press, 1993).

CHAPTER 11: DEITY

1. Pierre Teilhard de Chardin, *Christianity and Evolution*, trans. Rene Hague (New York: Harcourt Brace & Co., 1969), 240.

2. Teilhard de Chardin, *Hymn of the Universe*, 133.

3. Ibid., 77.

4. Ibid.

5. Pannenberg, *Faith and Reality*; and Peters, *God—the World's Future*.

6. See the more recent translation titled *The Human Phenomenon*, trans. Sarah Appleton-Weber (Portland, OR: Sussex Academic Press, 1999).

7. Ian Barbour, "Five Ways to Read Teilhard," *The Teilhard Review* 3 (1968): 3–20.

8. Monod, *Chance and Necessity*, 32.

9. See Stephen Jay Gould's essays in *Natural History* 88 (March 1979): 86–97; 89 (August 1980): 8–28; and 90 (June 1981): 12–30. For a refutation of Gould's uninformed and scurrilous attack on Teilhard, see Thomas King, SJ, "Teilhard and Piltdown," in Thomas King, SJ, and James Salmon, SJ, eds., *Teilhard and the Unity of Knowledge* (New York: Paulist Press, 1983), 159–69.

10. Dennett, *Darwin's Dangerous Idea*, 320.

11. Peter Medawar's review of *The Phenomenon of Man* that first appeared in *Mind* in 1961 is reprinted in *The Art of the Soluble* (London: Methuen, 1967), 71–81.

12. See B. Alan Wallace, *The Taboo of Subjectivity: Toward a New Science of Consciousness* (New York: Oxford University Press, 2000).

13. "If the cosmos were basically material," Teilhard writes, "it would be physically incapable of containing man. Therefore, we may conclude (and this is the first step) that it is in its inner being made *of spiritual stuff*." See Pierre Teilhard de Chardin, *Human Energy*, trans. J. M. Cohen (New York: Harvest Books/Harcourt Brace Jovanovich, 1962), 119–20.

14. Pierre Teilhard de Chardin, "The Mass on the World," in Thomas M. King, *Teilhard's Mass: Approaches to "The Mass on the World"* (New York: Paulist Press, 2005), 145–58.

15. Pierre Teilhard de Chardin, *The Future of Man,* trans. Norman Denny (New York: Harper Colophon Books, 1964), 83.

16. Teilhard, "The Mass on the World."

17. Ibid., 150.

18. Teilhard, *Human Energy*, 22.

Index